Spiritual Power
in
Your Teaching

Spiritual Power
in
Your Teaching

by

Roy B. Zuck

MOODY PRESS
CHICAGO

Original title: *The Holy Spirit*
in Your Teaching

Moody Press Revised Edition, 1972
Library of Congress Catalog Card No. 63-21391
ISBN: 0-8024-8216-3

The author gratefully acknowledges the kindness of the publisher in giving
permission to quote from EDUCATION THAT IS CHRISTIAN by Lois
E. LeBar. Copyright © 1958 by Fleming H. Revell Company.

Printed in the United States of America

Contents

Foreword

CHRISTIAN EDUCATION is essential, not optional. Embroidered into the fabric of New Testament Christianity is the command to teach.

Tragically, education in the Christian church has too often been equated with methods and materials, gadgets and gimmicks, to the exclusion of underlying philosophy and derived principles. It is indeed refreshing to find a basic text which sinks deep shafts into the bedrock of evangelical theology. Without theological substructure, Christian education cannot hope to be effective. Communication presupposes content.

For teachers, directors of Christian education, pastors — indeed any responsible person in the teaching ministry of the church — Dr. Zuck performs a notable service. In the elusive world of pedagogics there are some teachers whose instruction invariably produces healthy fruit. Students who have "had" such teachers have experienced spiritual growth. But what makes these teachers capable of preparing and serving scriptural truth so skillfully that it nourishes the hearts of the listeners, as well as trains their minds? Dr. Zuck furnishes thought-provoking answers to this question.

This study is basically an explanation of God's plan for relating the human teacher to the divine Teacher, the Holy Spirit. Those who are teaching biblical truth need to reflect on the person and work of the Holy Spirit, for their task is a most delicate and difficult one. Eternal issues are at stake.

7

The presumptuous pedagogue who presents spiritual truth on his own terms — however excellent may be his techniques — teaches in vain. He is like the man who tries to run his gasoline engine on water. It is powerless. No eternal grades are recorded for the class whose learning has been generated by the aqueous fuel of mere human instruction.

The author, in addition to possessing keen educational insights, is trained in a rich theological tradition, uniquely equipping him to combine two oft-divorced fields of study — theology and education. To counsel others on the teaching ministry of the Holy Spirit, one must have "been there," connected to the power line of divine energy, a witness to changed lives. This volume comes from such a teacher, who teaches God's Word in the power of the Spirit.

We are indebted to Dr. Zuck for this valuable contribution to the growing spate of Christian educational literature. May his seed fall on good ground and bring forth much fruit.

HOWARD G. HENDRICKS

Dallas Theological Seminary

Preface

TO MANY PEOPLE, Christian education means methods, materials, organizations, programs. Thus conceived, Christian education seems like something foisted on Christianity and foreign to anything theological or spiritual. Of course the work of Christian education does involve methods, materials, organizations, programs, and so on. But it is more than these. Simply defined, evangelical Christian education is the Christ-centered, Bible-based, pupil-related process of communicating God's written Word through the power of the Holy Spirit, for the purpose of leading pupils to Christ and building them up in Christ.

Defined in this way, evangelical Christian education is seen as a theological discipline — a work to be rooted deeply in and to be derived squarely from theological concepts and biblical truths. And it is a divine-human task, in which born-again teachers face the thrilling opportunity of cooperating with God, the Holy Spirit, as "workers together with him" (2 Co 6:1).

The purpose of this study is to demonstrate the need for the ministry of the Holy Spirit in Christian education, and to discuss how the Spirit works in the various phases of the teaching-learning process. It is written for teachers and other Christian education workers in local churches, and also for those engaged in Christian teaching in educational institutions on elementary, secondary, and higher levels, and in other church-related agencies.

I trust that this book will help bridge the rift that sometimes prevails between theology and Christian education, and that it will inspire teachers to give God's Spirit His rightful place in their educational ministries — and thus enjoy the divine dynamics of teaching!

This book is a revision of my doctoral dissertation presented to Dallas Theological Seminary in 1961. I am grateful to the administrative committee of the seminary for granting permission to publish the dissertation in book form. Gratitude is expressed to Dr. John F. Walvoord, president of Dallas Theological Seminary, and Dr. John A. Witmer, associate professor of systematic theology, for guidance in writing the dissertation. I also express deep appreciation to Professor Howard G. Hendricks, chairman of the department of Christian education, for introducing me to the exciting field of Christian education and to the subject of this book. My wife, Dorothy, is to be thanked for encouraging me in this work, and for her sacrificial assistance which helped make this book possible.

May God bless those teachers everywhere who, being taught by Him, faithfully commit God's precious Word to their pupils, so that they, in turn, may "be able to teach others also" (2 Ti 2:2).

In Teaching, I Am Taught

I heard the Father say, "Go teach,"
  And marveled at His call,
"I cannot others teach," said I,
  "For I am least of all."

"Though thou be least," the Father said,
  "Yet I have need of thee.
Where thou art weak, I am full strong,
  Thou canst do all through Me."

Since I have yielded to His call
  Whene'er His help I've sought
His Spirit fills my every need,
  In teaching, I am taught.

HAZEL M. LINDSEY

11

Introduction

Power in Your Teaching

I OFTEN WONDER if I'm *getting through* to my pupils."

"Why do I seem to have *so few results* in my teaching of the Bible? I seem to be getting nowhere."

"I feel that I'm making little or no *spiritual headway* in my class. Apparently my students aren't growing in the Lord."

Do these statements reflect your feelings, as a teacher of the Bible? Do you sense that you lack spiritual and dynamic effectiveness?

WHY "HEARERS ONLY"?

Why do so many pupils in evangelical churches seem unchallenged and unchanged by Bible teaching? Must you be content with lack of spiritual growth and maturity, with the absence of Christlike living? Can you do nothing to bridge the chasm that seems to exist between pupils' knowledge of the truth and their practice of it?

The teaching — and the learning — of God's Word *ought* to be an interesting, exuberant adventure. Communicating God's precious truth *ought* to result in transformed lives, and in pupils being "doers of the word and not hearers only" (Ja 1:22).* But too often Sunday school and other Bible-

---

*All Scripture references are taken from the American Standard Version (1901) unless otherwise indicated.

teaching classes are lifeless, uninteresting, the essence of boredom.

How do our young people leave their Sunday School classrooms on Sunday morning? With eyes sparkling, with new vision and insight? With serious determination to practice the will of God? With chin up, ready to face an unbelieving world in the power of the Spirit? With deep questions about God Himself? Too often they are glad for release from a dull, boring session.[1]

WHAT ARE THE DYNAMICS OF BIBLE TEACHING?

Pastors, teachers, youth leaders, and other church workers are becoming aware of the fact that Christianity is, to a large extent, educational. Increasingly, there is evidence of the resurgence of educational interest among Evangelicals. Church leaders are seeing that a balanced, coordinated, educational church program can help dispel pupil disinterest. Employing appropriate teaching techniques and using suitable instructional materials can be conducive to interesting teaching.

But these factors — important as they are — cannot, in themselves, guarantee teaching power.

Secular educators utilize these educational factors to good advantage, but one cannot say therefore that secular education possesses spiritual vitality. And even theologically liberal religious educators seek to use the best in teaching procedures and materials. But Evangelicals would not concede that liberal religious educators know much of the spiritual reality so necessary to transform pupils' lives toward Christlikeness. There must be something else that guarantees spiritual effectiveness in Bible teaching — and which at the same time makes evangelical Christian education distinctive from secular and liberal religious education.

The three indispensable factors that make Christian education dynamic, and at the same time distinctive, are: (1) the centrality of God's written revelation, (2) the necessity of regeneration, and (3) the ministry of the Holy Spirit. These are the *dynamics* of Christian education. The presence and functioning of these three together comprise a distinctive education, from the evangelical standpoint. To seek to have Christian education without the Word of God is to extricate the basic core of the curriculum. Unregenerate teachers cannot communicate, in the full sense of the word, Christian truths, which they themselves do not know experientially. And the Holy Spirit's work is necessary for spiritual enablement in every phase of teaching and learning.

THE CENTRALITY OF REVELATION

Without the Bible as the foundation and core of the curriculum, there can be no true Christian education. An adequate philosophy of Christian education must incorporate the basic concept of God's revelation of Himself to finite man through the medium of His written Word, the Bible. This is basic and essential.

Because of man's sinful, depraved condition, he is spiritually dead and does not know God (Ro 3:10-23; 1 Co 2: 14; 2 Co 4:4; Eph 2:1-2). Therefore, God has revealed Himself to men in various ways: in creation (which is referred to as "general revelation" and which reveals God's wisdom, power, and glory); in direct revelation (especially in Old Testament times, through dreams, visions, and the spoken word); in miracles; in Christ, the eternal, living Word (Jn 1:1, 14; 14:9-11); and in the written Word, God's scriptural revelation. Scripture, as "a mode of divine disclosure," is itself revelation.[2] "While the process of revelation is broader than the Bible, the content of special revelation is for us identical with the Biblical message."[3]

In evangelical Christian education, scriptural revelation is accepted as the Christian's supreme and final authority, the infallible guide to faith and practice, for three reasons.

First, scriptural revelation is of divine origin. Since God

has revealed Himself in permanent, written form, man need not search further for a source of knowledge about God and a means of experience with Him. His revelation is divinely inspired by the Holy Spirit (2 Ti 3:16; 2 Pe 1:20-21), and therefore infallible and authoritative.

The Bible is the "given" content, the authoritative norm for Christian education. It is essential to any ministry that seeks to teach others God's ways and will.

Second, God's written Word is basic in Christian education because it is the means of imparting divine life (1 Pe 1:23), and it is the source of Christian nurture and growth (1 Pe 2:2). A valid Christian experience (whether it be birth into the Christian life — regeneration; or growth within the Christian life — education) cannot be obtained or maintained apart from valid Christian truth, God's written revelation, the Bible.

If Christian experience or knowledge of God is sought from sources other than this revelation, then Christian education is decimated to a humanistic, anthropocentric religious education. In true Christian education, the Bible is the objective body of truth to which the experiences of pupils are to be related and by which the pupils' experiences are to be affected.

Third, scriptural revelation provides a standard by which man's experiences may be measured. Without the Bible as the foundation of Christian education, the experiences of learners are virtually immeasurable. Omit the Bible, and teachers have no objective basis or ground of evaluation by which to judge the validity of spiritual experiences. Without the Bible, teachers and pupils are left to their subjective, self-imposed standards. But with God's revelation as the evaluative standard, unsaved pupils are challenged to accept Christ as Saviour, and pupils who know the Lord are challenged to lead lives of holiness (1 Th 5:23; 1 Pe 1:15) and to mature into Christlikeness (Ro 8:29; 2 Co 3:18; Eph 4:12-13).

Therefore the place of written revelation is integral, not peripheral, to an educational philosophy that is distinctly Christian. The Bible is the infallible, objective body of truth essential to the transformation of lives, first in regeneration and then in the outliving of the indwelling Saviour.

THE NECESSITY OF REGENERATION

Without Christian teachers there can be no Christian teaching. Real Christian education is impossible where neither teacher nor pupil is Christian. Only teachers who are regenerated by the Spirit of God (Titus 3:5) and are thus born into God's family, begin to qualify to do Christian teaching.

To neglect this distinctive is to destroy the lines of demarcation between mere religious education and true Christian education, between liberal religious teaching and evangelical Christian teaching. Though liberals have advanced far in the field of education, they generally have given little attention to the spiritual qualifications of the teacher. This is to be expected. For it is in keeping with the theology of liberalism, which tends to deprecate the need for a conversion experience. All that most liberals require is that a teacher be religion-minded and have some kind of nebulously defined faith in God.

Neoliberals, however, are giving more heed to the sinful nature of man, the need for God's grace, and the reconciling work of Christ. Some liberal educators are now more concerned that their teaching be theologically oriented, but these emphases have done little as yet to cause liberal and neoliberal educators to see the new birth as a requisite for Christian teaching.

Education, to be distinctly Christian, must be conducted by persons who have been redeemed through faith in Jesus Christ, and who thus have a personal relationship to Him. Without the living reality of this experience of salvation through God's grace, a teacher is not a Christian, and his teaching can in no sense be called Christian teaching. This is true for several reasons:

First, the *aim* of Christian education necessitates born-again teachers. The transformation of lives, the growth of Christian personalities, the nurturing of pupils toward conformity to the will of God, demand that the teacher be one who possesses high spiritual objectives.

Second, the *nature* of Christian teaching demands regenerate instructors. Christian teaching is a divine calling, not simply a secular vocation. It is a ministry *divinely* ordained of God for the purpose of using *divinely* appointed persons to communicate truths of a *divinely* inspired Book, in order to help pupils lead *divine* lives.

Since the entire process is a divine one, only those who are divinely regenerated by God's Spirit qualify to engage in this ministry. An unsaved man, though religious, does not know God and therefore is incapable of communicating the truth and will of God to others.

Third, the *influence* of teachers' lives demands that teachers know Christ in salvation. The life, words, actions, attitudes, convictions, and objectives of the teacher all influence his pupils to one degree or another. A teacher who does not know Christ as Saviour is unable to influence his pupils with the realities of his own Christian life, because he has none. God's plan is to teach through regenerated personalities whom He indwells.

THE MINISTRY OF THE HOLY SPIRIT

Christian education demands using the Word of God and only born-again instructors, but even these do not guarantee that Christian teaching will be spirtually effective.

The Holy Spirit, working through the Word of God, is the spiritual dynamic for Christian living. If the Holy Spirit is not at work through the teacher and through the written Word of God, then Christian education remains virtually in-

effective and is little different from secular teaching. Murray
stresses the sterility of Christianity apart from the Holy Spirit:

> The reason that there is so much Bible reading and teach-
> ing which has no power to elevate and sanctify the life is
> simply this: it is not truth which has been revealed and re-
> ceived through the Holy Spirit.[4]

Murch very pointedly decries the insipid condition of
much Christian teaching:

> The average church school of our day overlooks the divine
> element in Christian education. It is a slave to cold propo-
> sitions, to methods and programs which are purely intel-
> lectual in concept. Thus it lacks divine warmth and passion.
> . . . It fails to give the spiritual dynamic for Christian liv-
> ing.[5]

But why is the Holy Spirit's ministry so essential in a process that is basically educational? Cannot regenerate teachers utilizing a Bible-structured curriculum be known as educators who are Christian? If a prepared teacher follows
sound pedagogical principles, uses proper teaching methods,
is interested in his pupils, and operates with and within a
curriculum based on the Bible, does not that comprise true
Christian teaching? Emphatically no! A number of facts
make the ministry of the Holy Spirit essential to dynamic
Bible teaching:

First, the work of God's Spirit in the lives of regenerate
teachers is needed so that they may be effective instruments
in the hands of God. God's servants must be properly adjusted to the Spirit of God. The powerless, ineffective, carnal
living of many believers attests to the fact that being rightly
related to Christ (in salvation) does not necessarily mean
being rightly related to the Holy Spirit (in spirituality).
Salvation and spirituality are two different matters. One is
saved when he places faith in Christ; one is "spiritual" when
he is yielded to and filled by God's Spirit (Gal 5:16; Eph
5:18). One who is saved may at once yield to God and be

spiritual; but too often after salvation, Christians lead carnal lives, unyielded to God.

Effectiveness in service, after one is saved, depends on yieldedness to the Holy Spirit. Service done in the energy of the flesh — including even the ministry of teaching — is of little avail.

Too often Christian teachers fail to allow for the Spirit's guidance, enablement, and enlightenment as they prepare and as they teach. Thus they are hardly different from unsaved teachers in secular education who know of no such available source of enablement. Unregenerate teachers have no spiritual resources; Christian teachers have spiritual resources but often fail to use them!

How can pupils be led into lives of fellowship with God, if their teachers know nothing of the joy of such fellowship attained by the Spirit's filling? Dynamic Spirit-filled living on a high spiritual plane is God's attainable ideal for every Christian teacher.

Second, the Holy Spirit's ministry is needed so that the Word of God may be made effectual in pupils' lives. The Holy Spirit and the written Word of God work in conjunction.

But some may object to this thought by saying that the Bible is an energetic, animated Book, able to energize, redeem, empower, and enlighten by itself, without the accompanying ministry of the Holy Spirit.

True, the Bible *is* a living, powerful Book. Twice in Scripture the Word of God is described as "living." Hebrews 4:12 states that the Bible is "quick" or "living," and 1 Peter 1:23 also declares it to be "living." And twice in Scripture the Word of God is described as "energetic." Hebrews 4:12 contains the adjective *powerful,* which comes from the Greek word meaning "energetic." 1 Thessalonians 2:13 speaks of the Word of God as that "which also worketh [energizes] in you that believe."

Being God-breathed and verbally inspired, the Bible has

divine life resident in it. Thus it has power to generate faith (Ps 19:7; Ro 10:17; 2 Ti 3:15; Ja 1:18; 1 Pe 1:23), to sanctify and nurture (Jn 17:17-19; Ac 20:32; Eph 5: 26; 1 Pe 2:2), and to enlighten (Ps 119:105, 130; 2 Ti 3:16). Its supernatural power, its animating vitality must not be underestimated. In fact, this animation is one reason why scriptural revelation stands as an essential divine element in Christian education.

However, as all of Scripture is taken into consideration, it becomes evident that the Holy Spirit and the Word of God operate together. The Holy Spirit's ministry is essential for any proper reception of the truth (1 Co 2:12-15; Eph 1: 17-18). The Holy Spirit, along with the Word, is said to regenerate (Jn 3:5-7; Titus 3:5), to sanctify (2 Th 2:13; 1 Pe 1:2) and to enlighten (Jn 14:26, 16:13; 1 Co 2: 10-15).

Therefore, it is obvious that "the written Word . . . is always indissolubly joined with the power of the Holy Spirit."[6] However, these questions must be considered: What is the relation of these two? Why cannot the Word of God be efficacious by itself?

An answer may be obtained by distinguishing between the "resident life" of the Scriptures themselves and their "operative efficaciousness." The Bible has life, but it does not always *beget* life. Only when the operative power of the Spirit accompanies the Word is it efficacious.

This is verified both by experience and scriptural revelation. Not all who hear the Word believe (e.g., Jn 10:25, 12:47-48; Ac 7:57-59; 17:5, 32). Many who hear the truth are not regenerated because the Spirit of God has not so used the Word to make it efficacious to their salvation. Hodge points out that for the Word of God to regenerate, the Holy Spirit must supernaturally (and simultaneously, it should be added) remove the spiritual blindness of unbelievers to enable them to receive the saving power of the Word (2 Co 4:3-4; Jn 16:7-11).[7]

Also, many believers are not growing by means of the Word — though they hear the Word — because their carnal condition prohibits the Holy Spirit from making the Word and its truths operative in their lives (1 Co 3:1-3; Heb 5: 12-14).

The efficacy of the Word depends on the Holy Spirit's ministry. Wallace states that "the Word of God can have no efficacy unless at the same time the Holy Spirit works in the hearts of the hearers, creating faith and making men's minds open to receive the Word."[8] And, in relation to man's receptivity, he quotes Calvin, "The heavenly doctrine proves to be useful and efficacious to us only so far as the Spirit both forms our minds to understand it and our hearts to submit to its yoke."[9]

Therefore, in both salvation and Christian living the Holy Spirit's ministry is essential. Though the Bible is "living" and "energetic" (Heb 4:12), it is not efficaciously operative without the Spirit's ministry. The Scriptures accomplish their purposes to the extent that learners appropriate the Word by the Holy Spirit. The question then is not that of the inherent power of the Word — that is granted; but of the Holy Spirit's appropriation of the Word to individuals' hearts and lives.

It is obvious, then, that Christian education cannot afford to neglect the place of the ministry of the Spirit, as human teachers seek to communicate the Bible to pupils and as pupils seek to appropriate it personally.

These three emphases — revelation, regeneration, and the Holy Spirit — are basic to an adequate philosophy of Christian education. To neglect them, or any one of them, is to fail to have true *Christian* education. Only with all three can teachers begin to experience something of the divine dynamics of Christian teaching.

Part 1

THE BIBLICAL DOCTRINE OF
THE HOLY SPIRIT AS A TEACHER

What does the Bible say about the Holy Spirit as a Teacher? How does His teaching ministry relate to His other ministries? How are certain difficult passages about the Spirit's place in teaching to be understood?

Knowing what the Bible teaches about the divine Teacher Himself will help teachers know better how to depend on and cooperate with Him as they teach God's Word.

1

The Titles of the Spirit as a Teacher

BIEDERWOLF POINTS OUT that fifty-two designations are ascribed to the Holy Spirit in the entire Word of God.[1] Of these, at least seven relate to His work of teaching: Spirit of wisdom, Spirit of wisdom and understanding, Spirit of counsel and might, Spirit of knowledge and of the fear of Jehovah, Spirit of truth, Paraclete, Spirit of wisdom and revelation.

SPIRIT OF WISDOM

This title "Spirit of wisdom" occurs first in Exodus 28:3, where God commands Moses to secure "wisehearted" tailors, "whom I have filled with the spirit of wisdom," to make priestly garments. The Holy Spirit was the source of divine wisdom for these tailors, which enabled them to perform their tasks nobly.

Bezaleel was "filled . . . with the Spirit of God" (Ex 31:3), and as a result, Bezaleel had wisdom, understanding, and knowledge for his craftsmanship (Ex 31:3-5, 35:31-35). This filling also gave him the ability to teach his crafts to others (Ex 35:34).

SPIRIT OF WISDOM AND UNDERSTANDING

"Spirit of wisdom and understanding" is the first of three pairs of titles ascribed to the Spirit of Jehovah in Isaiah

25

11:2. Christ, the "shoot out of the stock of Jesse" (Is 11:1) was equipped by God's Spirit for His great earthly ministry. The Spirit of God "rested" (literally, settled down) on Him, and as a result, Christ possessed wisdom, understanding, counsel, might, knowledge, and the fear of the Lord. These are gifts given by the Spirit to Christ, and apparently are given to some extent by the Spirit to Christian teachers today.

Only one Spirit descends on Christ (a singular verb is used), but the Spirit is designated by several different titles because He bestows several different benefits.

"The first pair relates to the intellectual life, the second to the practical life, and the third to the direct relation to God."[2] The Hebrew word for wisdom suggests prudence, and the word for understanding suggests discernment and perception. It is interesting that a form of the Hebrew word for understanding is translated "teacher" in Ezra 8:16.

SPIRIT OF COUNSEL AND MIGHT

This title of the Holy Spirit, "Spirit of counsel and might," in Isaiah 11:2 depicts His ability to impart the gift of forming proper plans (or giving proper advice) and of carrying them out with physical energy. The word *counsel* suggests the ability to provide good advice, and the word *might* suggests the ability to carry out that counsel. Of course, the Holy Spirit enabled Christ to carry on His earthly ministry of teaching by supplying Him with counsel and energy. The Spirit seeks to provide similar counsel and insight, might and strength to Christian teachers today.

SPIRIT OF KNOWLEDGE AND OF THE FEAR OF JEHOVAH

The Holy Spirit also supplied Christ with "knowledge and the fear of Jehovah." Though "the fear of Jehovah is the beginning [starting point] of knowledge" (Pr 1:7), the fact that this title occurs last in Isaiah 11:2 indicates that the fear of the Lord is also the end result of knowledge. True knowledge must begin with and result in reverence for God. The Holy Spirit seeks to supply Christian teachers with both knowledge and godly reverence, two inseparable requisites for effective teaching of God's Word.

From these three titles of the Holy Spirit in Isaiah 11:2, it is clear that Christ was specially endowed by the Holy Spirit with prudence, discernment, counsel, strength, knowledge, and reverence for Jehovah. Such can be the portion of born-again instructors today, too, as they depend on the Spirit for His enabling.

SPIRIT OF TRUTH

The title "Spirit of truth" occurs three times in the Bible and only in John's gospel: John 14:17, 15:26, and 16:13. Some writers suggest that this title means that the Holy Spirit is "the true Spirit" or "the truthful Spirit." Others say that the title indicates that the Holy Spirit bears witness to Christ, who is the Truth.[3]

But the contexts of the above verses, particularly the context of John 16:13, support the idea that the title, "Spirit of truth," refers to the Spirit as the *source* of truth. "When he, the Spirit of truth, is come, he shall guide you into all the truth" (Jn 16:13). And closely related to this is the thought that He is the Spirit of truth because He *applies* the truth to believers' lives. The Spirit can apply the truth only by virtue of the fact that He is the source of truth. Many commentators hold to this view. For example, Lange states that "He is the Spirit of truth, inasmuch as He makes objective truth subjective in believers."[4]

Christian teachers may present God's truths to pupils, but only the Spirit of truth can impart and appropriate those truths personally to pupils' hearts.

PARACLETE

The word *Paraclete,* which is an English transliteration of the Greek, occurs five times in the New Testament, all in the writings of John. The references are John 14:16, 26; 15:26; 16:7; and 1 John 2:1. In the gospel of John the word speaks of the Holy Spirit; in the epistle of John it is used of Christ. In the King James and American Standard Versions the word is translated "Comforter" in the gospel of John and "Advocate" in 1 John. The verses in the American Standard Version read thus:

> And I will pray the Father, and he shall give you another Comforter, that he may be with you for ever, even the Spirit of truth: whom the world cannot receive; for it beholdeth him not, neither knoweth him: ye know him; for he abideth with you, and shall be in you (Jn 14:16-17).

> But the Comforter, even the Holy Spirit, whom the Father will send in my name, he shall teach you all things, and bring to your remembrance all that I said unto you (Jn 14:26).

> But when the Comforter is come, whom I will send unto you from the Father, even the Spirit of truth, which proceedeth from the Father, he shall bear witness of me (Jn 15:26).

> Nevertheless I tell you the truth: It is expedient for you that I go away; for if I go not away, the Comforter will not come unto you; but if I go, I will send him unto you (Jn 16:7).

> My little children, these things write I unto you that ye may not sin. And if any man sin, we have an Advocate with the Father, Jesus Christ the righteous (1 Jn 2:1).

These verses indicate that the Paraclete was given by the Father (Jn 14:16), was sent by the Father (14:26), proceeds from the Father (15:26), and was sent by the Son (15:26, 16:7). He came to be with the disciples forever

(14:16), to indwell them (14:17), to bear witness of Christ (15:26), and to convict the world (16:8).

Writers differ on which English word best translates the term *Paraclete*. The translation "Comforter" was the meaning that the Greek fathers ordinarily attached to the word (for example, Origen, Epiphanius, Chrysostom, Cyril of Jerusalem, and Gregory of Nyssa). Wycliffe and Tyndale were two of the first modern translators to use the rendering "Comforter," under the influence of the Latin Vulgate translation made by Jerome.

In classical Greek the word is used of a legal advocate or defender of the accused. Demosthenes used the word *advocates* of personal friends pleading before a judge on behalf of their accused friend to decide in his favor.[5]

Also Philo employs the word in several instances in the sense of advocate or intercessor. Philo writes about Joseph bestowing righteousness on his brethren who had wronged him and declaring that they needed no one else as "paraclete" or intercessor.[6]

There seems to be little doubt that the word *Paraclete* should be translated "Advocate" in 1 John 2:1. When Christians sin, Christ pleads their case before the heavenly Father. He is the Christian's Intercessor.

But the question is, How should *Paraclete* be translated when it refers to the Holy Spirit?

Some writers prefer the meaning of legal advocate and explain that the Spirit pleads Christ's cause with the believer.[7] But the statements about the Holy Spirit in John 14-16 do not suggest this view. Such a view does not include the many ministries that Christ said the Paraclete would undertake.[8]

Perhaps the best rendering of *Paraclete* when it refers to the Holy Spirit is "Helper." This seems to be better than the translation "Comforter" for four reasons.

First, the Greek word is a passive form, not an active form. Literally the word means "one who is called alongside," not "one who calls alongside of." Obviously, then, one who is called alongside to help is a "helper."

Second, to speak of the Spirit (as Christ did in Jn 14: 16) as "another Comforter" would imply that Christ too was a Comforter. This limits the concept of who Christ is, for He is far more than a Comforter.

Third, as the word developed in usage, it came to mean "a helper in general." A legal advocate who defends is one who helps by counseling, instructing, exhorting, helping, and attending to the defendant's personal interests.

Fourth, "Helper" designates an inclusive ministry, clearly indicated by the contexts of the passages in which Christ used the term. He says that the Paraclete will show the disciples the things of Christ; teach them things to come; teach them all things; refresh their memories about past teaching; bear witness to Christ; indwell believers; convict of sin, righteousness, and judgment; and will be given and sent by the Father to console the disciples in Christ's absence and to continue Christ's work. (However, the thought of advocating and comforting need not be excluded from the meaning of the term. *Helper* here may well embrace the thought of helping by interceding as an advocate and helping by giving comfort.)

The Holy Spirit is "one called alongside" to be the Helper of believers in every situation. He helps as their Defender, as their Comforter, as their Teacher, as their Protector, as their Counselor, as their Guide, as their Exhorter. He stands by them and renders any needed assistance.[9] He occupies Himself with the interests, comforts, needs, difficulties, ignorances, trials, and temptations of every child of God.

The fact that the Paraclete is equated three times with the Spirit of truth (Jn 14:17, 15:26, 16:13) shows that teaching is one aspect of the Paraclete's helping ministry. As the believers' Paraclete, the Holy Spirit is their Support in weaknesses, their Counselor in difficulties, their Consoler in afflictions, their Teacher in ignorance.

SPIRIT OF WISDOM AND REVELATION

Regarding the title "Spirit of wisdom and revelation," there is difference of opinion as to whether *spirit* in Ephesians 1:17 (where Paul prays that "the Father of glory may give unto you the spirit of wisdom and revelation in the knowledge of him," KJV) refers to the human spirit or the Holy Spirit.

Those who suggest that it means man's spirit give this translation: "the Father of glory may give unto you a wise spirit and revelation." But the major objection to this view is that revelation cannot be thought of as a gift given to man for discerning or *understanding* mysteries. Rather, it means a *disclosing* of mysteries. Revelation is the work of God by which He discloses truth to man, not an ability given by God to man for comprehending truth.

The more acceptable view of Ephesians 1:17 takes wisdom and revelation as gifts given by the Holy Spirit. One is the gift for general spiritual understanding, while the other is the gift of special revelation in particular.[10] Paul's prayer was that believers through the Holy Spirit would understand spiritual things and see the "full knowledge" of God.

These seven titles add support to the scriptural evidence of the personality and deity of the Spirit. The quality of personality, the possession of understanding, the position of divine Teacher, Revealer, Guide, and Instructor can all be based on these interesting titles ascribed to the third Person of the Trinity. Just the title Paraclete alone suffices to point to the personality of the Spirit.

As a Teacher, He makes others wise; gives understanding, counsel, strength, knowledge, and the fear of the Lord; imparts and appropriates truth; helps in every learning situation; provides for spiritual wisdom; and discloses knowledge regarding God.

2

The Teaching Ministries of the Spirit

SOMETHING of the exact nature of the Spirit's teaching tasks may be determined by examining the passages which speak of His instructing, reminding, guiding, declaring, and revealing. The relevant passages are these:

> But the Comforter [Helper], even the Holy Spirit, whom the Father will send in my name, he shall teach you all things, and bring to your remembrance all that I said unto you (Jn 14:26).
>
> I have yet many things to say unto you, but ye cannot bear them now. Howbeit when he, the Spirit of truth, is come, he shall guide you into all the truth: for he shall not speak from himself; but what things soever he shall hear, these shall he speak: and he shall declare unto you the things that are to come. He shall glorify me: for he shall take of mine, and shall declare it unto you. All things whatsoever the Father hath are mine: therefore said I, that he taketh of mine, and shall declare it unto you (Jn 16: 12-15).
>
> But unto us God revealed them through the Spirit: for the Spirit searcheth all things, yea, the deep things of God. For who among men knoweth the things of a man, save the spirit of the man, which is in him? Even so the things of God none knoweth, save the Spirit of God. But we received, not the spirit of the world, but the spirit which is

from God; that we might know the things that were freely given to us of God. Which things also we speak, not in words which man's wisdom teacheth, but which the Spirit teacheth; combining spiritual things with spiritual words (1 Co 2:10-13).

A scanning of the verbs in these verses reveals that the Holy Spirit instructs, brings to remembrance, guides, declares, and reveals. These promises of divine instruction pertain to several areas: (1) instruction in "all things" (Jn 14:26); (2) recollection of past utterances of Christ (14:26); (3) guidance into "all the truth" (16:13); (4) declaration of future events (16:13); and (5) revelation of the "deep things" of God (1 Co 2:10).

What does the Spirit teach? Whom does He teach? What does He bring to remembrance? How does He guide? What does He declare? What does He reveal? Let us examine these verses to see how the Holy Spirit specifically conducts His teaching ministry.

THE HOLY SPIRIT INSTRUCTS

The word translated "teach" in John 14:26 carries the meaning of instructing, delivering a discourse, explaining truth. In John 14:26, its indirect object *you* and its direct object *all things* point out the relevant, active nature of imparting truth from one person (the teacher) to other persons (the pupils). The teaching of the Holy Spirit involves content or truth (*all things*) and is directed toward persons (*you*). But to whom does *you* refer? And what is meant by *all things?*

Some interpreters endeavor to limit the word *you* to the few disciples who were with Christ on earth, without seeking to assign any direct application of the Spirit's teaching to Christians today. But parallel passages indicate otherwise. In the very same chapter (Jn 14:17), *the world* is said to be incapable of receiving, beholding, or knowing the Spirit of truth. If the world cannot receive the Spirit and His truths, then the implication is that all those who are *not* of the world, that is, all believers, *are* capable of receiving His truths. In the same verse the promise of Christ that the Spirit "shall be *in* you" clearly refers to all believers, for they are all indwelt by the Spirit (Ro 8:9; 2 Co 1:22; 1 Jn 3:24). The fact that "the natural man receiveth not the things of the Spirit of God" (1 Co 2:14) indicates that someone other than the "natural" or unsaved man *can* receive them.

However, though all believers are potentially capable of receiving the teaching of the Spirit, not all actually do, because the things of God are revealed by the Spirit only to *spiritual* (Spirit-filled) Christians.[1] That there are two classes of Christians, some carnal and others spiritual, is clear from 1 Corinthians 3:1, which is in a letter addressed to Corinthians who were Christians but were carnal: "And I, brethren, could not speak unto you as unto spiritual, but as unto carnal."

Only "spiritual" Christians who are manifesting the fruit of the Spirit (Gal 5:22), walking in the Spirit (Gal 5:16), and filled with the Spirit (Eph 5:18) can receive "the things of the Spirit of God . . . because they are spiritually judged. But he that is spiritual judgeth all things, and he himself is judged of no man" (1 Co 2:14-15). The word translated "judgeth" is an Athenian law term meaning "to discern or examine," and refers to a preliminary examination before a judge. "The unspiritual are out of court as religious critics."[2] Carnality vitiates the Christian's spiritual judgment and dulls him to the teaching ministry of the Holy Spirit. The *you,* then, refers to spiritual Christians, that is, believers in fellowship with Christ.

The words *all things* (Jn 14:26; 1 Co 2:10; 1 Jn 2: 20, 27) and *all the truth* (Jn 16:13) are puzzling because it is difficult to comprehend how the Holy Spirit teaches *every* kind of universal knowledge to spiritual believers. Yet the word *all* is used without reservation. But if the *all things* refer to scientific, universal knowledge, this would mean that Spirit-filled Christians could claim omniscience. This, in turn, would suggest that human teachers are unnecessary. Many writers see in the words *all things* the fullness of Christian knowledge regarding the plan of salvation. However, there is warrant for expanding the meaning beyond simply salvation or redemption truth to the broader concept of "all that belongs to the sphere of spiritual truth (so that) nothing that is essential to the knowledge of God or the guidance of life shall be wanting."[3] Such a broad concept is based on parallel phrases found elsewhere in Scripture. "What things soever he shall hear, these shall he speak" (Jn 16:13) indicates that the Spirit speaks only of the things He hears, and the things that He hears are explained as "all things whatsoever the Father hath" and the things that are "mine" (Christ's) (Jn 16:14-15). The *all things* that the Spirit searches are not universal knowledge but "the deep things of God" and "the things that were freely given to us of God" (1 Co 2:10, 12). These are also the things of which Paul speaks (2:13). Obviously these things do not refer to all areas of life and truth, and yet they are more than simply salvation truths. They are all truths pertaining to God and His person and program. Knowledge of God and the full body of revealed truth is imparted by the Spirit to those Christians who are spiritually receptive to His teaching. "All *the* truth" (as the Greek literally reads) is not encyclopedic truth in general but all *revealed* truth, recorded in God's written Word.

The word for teach or instruct which is used in John 14:26, is also used in 1 Corinthians 2:13. The verse reads, "Which things also we speak, not in words which man's wisdom teacheth, but which the Spirit teacheth; combining spiritual things with spiritual words." The "which things also we speak" are the "things that were freely given to us of God" (2:12), things that believers know because they have received "the Spirit which is from God." These are "the things of God" (2:11), the things that God has "prepared for them that love Him" (2:9). Christians speak, then, the revealed things of God "not in human-wisdom-taught words, but in (words) Spirit taught" (as the Greek text actually reads). Paul claims that the work of the Holy Spirit in revealing truths extends to the words. Spiritual truth *revealed* by the Spirit (2:10) is spoken in spiritual words *taught* by the Spirit (2:13).*[4]

THE HOLY SPIRIT REMINDS

The ministry of reminding is ascribed to the Spirit in only one verse, John 14:26, which also mentions the Spirit's teaching ministry: "But the Comforter, even the Holy Spirit, whom the Father will send in my name, he shall teach you all things, and bring to your remembrance all that I said unto you."

After Christ's departure, the Holy Spirit was to stimulate the minds of the disciples to recall the oral teachings and utterances of their Lord. "These things have I spoken unto you," Christ said, "while yet abiding with you" (Jn 14:25).

This ministry guaranteed the inerrancy of the apostles' inspired writing of the gospels. But, in addition to that, it was a part of the Spirit's teaching ministry to the disciples.

Many of the things that Christ spoke to His disciples had been forgotten by them. Also, very much of what He said was not comprehended at the time, and so would be more easily forgotten (cf. Mk 9:32; Jn 2:22, 12:16). Many of Jesus' utterances were obscure to His disciples because of their lack of sufficient spiritual background. "I have yet

---

*This is good support for believing that the inspiration of Scripture extends to words, that inspiration is verbal. If the phrase beginning with the word *combining* be taken to mean "combining spiritual ideas with spiritual words," then this fits the idea that spiritual concepts in revelation are combined with (put into, expressed by) spiritual words in inspiration.

many things to say unto you, but ye cannot bear them now" (Jn 16:12).

As the Spirit reminded the disciples of Christ's sayings, He then taught them their meanings. "These things understood not his disciples at the first: but when Jesus was glorified, then remembered they . . . these things" (Jn 12:16).

Obviously, believers today are not reminded of Christ's oral sayings as such, because they did not hear them. But Christians *are* reminded by the Spirit of the *recorded* sayings of Christ that are written in the gospels. And, of course, the teaching of the Spirit goes beyond just those recorded sayings of Christ. The Spirit of truth guides into *all* the truth (Jn 16:13) — all the written Word of God.

THE HOLY SPIRIT GUIDES

The term for *guide* in John 16:13 literally means "lead the way." It presents the Holy Spirit as a Guide who leads travelers into unknown territory. A guide directs or leads others into paths previously unfamiliar to them. This is the thought brought out in the previous verse (Jn 16:12). The disciples were unfamiliar with some truth; they needed the Holy Spirit to lead them into it.

Coming to know or understand truth is frequently depicted in Scripture as taking place with the help of a guide. Teaching is thought of as "leading the way." In Acts 8:31 the Ethiopian eunuch asks, "How can I [understand what I read], except some one shall guide me?" Guidance was needed so that he could comprehend the truth of what he read. And the psalmist requested that God lead him into God's truth and that God teach him (Ps 25:5).

The Holy Spirit, Christ promised, would guide — not drive or compel — believers into all the truth. The order of the Greek words emphasizes the adjective *all* and implies two things: (1) the Holy Spirit does not stress one truth at the expense of all others, and (2) the Spirit guides into all truth, whereas Christ revealed only a portion of what He would like to have unfolded. The Spirit is now completing what Christ "began both to do and to teach" (Ac 1:1). He is clarifying and amplifying what Christ had given in germ form, and He is unfolding what Christ had withheld.

The Holy Spirit does not unfold new revelations beyond the boundaries of Christ's teachings or of the Bible. This is clear from the statement in John 16:13 that "he shall not speak from himself; but what things soever he shall hear, these shall he speak." He shows those things that He has received from Christ (16:15).

This does not mean, as some suppose, that the Spirit does not speak *about* Himself. Rather, He does not speak *from* Himself, independently of the Father and the Son. The Father, the Son, and the Spirit are one in essence. Therefore, what the Spirit hears from the Father (16:13) and takes from the Son (16:15), He communicates to believers.

What the Spirit hears is obviously in keeping with what Christ desired to teach the disciples. As He guides, the Holy Spirit enlarges on what Christ taught, without teaching independently of the Father and the Son. Not speaking from Himself, He guides believers into what He hears and receives, namely, all the truth, all the revelation of God.†

But are all believers automatically led by the Spirit into all the truth? Obviously not, for guidance implies obedience to the Guide and a willingness to be led. Believers may advance and grow in the grace and knowledge of the Lord Jesus Christ only as they are willing to be guided by the Holy Spirit, their divine Teacher.

_____

†Some Bible commentators believe that the guidance of the Spirit here in Jn 16:13 refers to the Spirit's work of inspiration, leading the disciples in writing New Testament books. However, Jn 16:13 seems to be directed to all Christians (as in the entire Upper Room discourse, Jn 14-16). Also, the word *guide* is a more apt figure of instructing than of inspiring (see Ac 8:31 and Ps 25:5). In addition, it seems unlikely that Christ was addressing the disciples about writing inspired Scripture because most of the twelve did *not* write New Testament books.

THE HOLY SPIRIT DECLARES

Declaring or announcing things to come is another phase of the teaching work of the third Person of the Godhead. In John 16:13-14, the verb for *declare* occurs two times: "He will declare to you things to come"; "He shall take of mine, and shall declare it unto you."

What is meant by *the things that are coming* (the Greek has the present tense)?

Some writers suggest that the verse is a promise to the disciples that they would write about the future under the Spirit's inspiration. But if this were the case, *announce* or *declare* is hardly the verb to be expected. Just as the recalling of Christ's oral utterances is not to be identified with the inspiration of the gospels, so the announcing of things that are coming is not to be identified with the inspiration of the epistles and the Apocalypse.

Several expositors assume that *the things that are coming* refers to prophecies of future events at the time of Christ's return. Others[5] suggest that the words meant *to the disciples* the things that were soon to come in the new age of grace — in the near as well as the not-so-near future — rather than *exclusively* the last days at the time of Christ's second coming.

Does the Spirit do this work for believers today? Yes, He does this by illuminating in their minds and hearts what God has already revealed in His Word about His program for the world and for present-day Christian living. These are the things, Christ said, that are "of mine." What to Christ's disciples were "things that are coming" are to believers today "things that are present"; that is, all that is revealed in the New Testament about God's workings in this present age. The Holy Spirit teaches believers these things from His holy Word. This is a major part of His teaching ministry.

The Holy Spirit Reveals

The truth of God, unknown by men who have not experienced God's salvation, is revealed by the Holy Spirit to those who love God. As Paul states, "But as it is written, Things which eye saw not, and ear heard not, And which entered not into the heart of man, Whatsoever things God prepared for them that love him. But unto us God revealed them through the Spirit" (1 Co 2:9-10).

Walvoord makes this pointed observation about this passage:

> Here is an epistemology that transcends the human senses. God is known by a process that does not involve the eye or the ear, nor does it originate in the heart, or human consciousness. Here is a frontal denial of empiricism, the idea that all knowledge comes through the senses. Knowledge comes through the ministry of the Holy Spirit of God.[6]

The Holy Spirit is the instrument through whom God reveals to Christians the "things God prepared" (1 Co 2:9), "the deep things of God" which the Spirit searches (2:10), "the things . . . freely given to us of God" (2:12), and "the things of the Spirit of God" (2:14).

Because the Holy Spirit comprehends the depths of God's nature, He is competent to reveal the things of God to man. The verses that follow in 1 Corinthians 2 expound this fact in further detail by the analogy of man's spirit and God's Spirit. As only the spirit of man truly knows man, so only the Spirit of God truly knows God (2:11).

But if only the Holy Spirit knows God, how can *man* know God? The answer is, by the Spirit of God whom believers have received (2:12). He reveals God and His truths to "them that love him" (2:9).

No man can know the plans, thoughts, and intentions of another man unless that man chooses to reveal them. So it is with God. No one can know His plans and designs unless

He chooses to make them known by His Spirit. And such He has chosen to do. Having received the Spirit of God at salvation, Christians may know, as the Spirit teaches them, "the things . . . of God" (2:12).

The word for *know* in 1 Corinthians 2:12 suggests that, because of the teaching work of the indwelling Holy Spirit, believers possess an inherent knowledge of the things of God revealed in His Word — things that eye, ear, and heart are unable to know or comprehend through seeing, hearing, or feeling. How privileged are Christians to know through God's Spirit and God's Word something of the very heart, nature, and plans of God!

3

Ministries of the Spirit
Related to Teaching

SEVERAL OTHER MINISTRIES of the Spirit are closely related
to His work of teaching. They are inspiration, conviction,
indwelling, and illumination.

INSPIRATION AND TEACHING

Inspiration is that supernatural work of the Holy Spirit
whereby He so guided and superintended the writers of
Scripture that what they wrote is the Word of God, inerrant
as originally written (2 Pe 1:21). The personality and
style of the writers were not obliterated by this action of the
Holy Spirit. This "breathing" of God (2 Ti 3:16) into the
writings was an act both verbal (the Spirit guided in the
choice of the words — which cannot be separated from
thoughts) and plenary (inspiration extended to every portion of the Bible so that it is infallible in truth and final in
authority).

Inspiration differs from teaching in the following ways:

First, only the writers of Scripture were involved in the
Spirit's work of inspiration, whereas *all* believers may receive the Spirit's teaching. In the statement, "all Scripture
is God-breathed," in 2 Timothy 3:16, there is no implica-

tion that any believers other than the human authors of Scripture were used by God in inspiration.

2 Peter 1:21 states the method that the Spirit employed in the act of inspiration. The writers were "borne along" by the Spirit, much as a sailboat is borne along by the wind. The Bible never suggests that any people other than those holy men of God who were superintended to pen the words of Scripture are "borne along" by the Spirit. The fact that the canon of Scripture is closed indicates that the Spirit is no longer speaking through human authors to inspire new words of Scripture. As demonstrated previously in chapter 2, Christ was addressing *all* believers, not just the disciples, when He stated in John 14:26 and 16:13 that "He shall teach *you* all things" and "He shall guide *you* into all the truth." Certainly, while no mature Christian would claim to be guided by the Spirit of God to write biblical revelation beyond that of the limits of the scriptural canon, many believers can attest that God's Spirit has guided them into understanding and appropriating revealed truth, the faith once for all delivered to the saints.

Second, inspiration was an act once for all completed when the Spirit composed the sixty-sixth book of Scripture. The Holy Spirit no longer has a ministry of inspiration; the act is past, and the canon is complete. On the other hand, the Holy Spirit is presently engaged in a continuous ministry of instruction. The departure of Christ into heaven enabled the Spirit to come and minister in His stead (Jn 14:16-19, 26; 16:7, 13, 16). The fact that Christ is still positioned in heaven is clear indication that the Holy Spirit is still carrying on in Christ's absence as His "substitute Teacher."

Third, inspiration is the act of God the Spirit in which He caused writers to *record* God's revelation. Thus, in a sense, inspiration is revelation, an unveiling. However, to be precise, in inspiration the human authors were used of God to seal in writing the truth which God at the time was unveiling about Himself in words. The Bible *is* revelation (not only a record of revelation), and inspiration was the act whereby God put the revealed truths into infallible written form. Revelation is the communication of truth which would not otherwise be known, whereas inspiration is the process whereby this information is presented accurately in written language. Revelation is the Spirit's disclosure of divine truth, whereas inspiration is the Spirit's superintending process of recording His revelation.

In Scripture the two sometimes converge. This is why they are sometimes confused. Revelation sometimes occurred without inspiration, as illustrated in Exodus 20:22 and Revelation 10:4. And inspiration sometimes did not involve the revealing of a new, previously unveiled truth, as seen in 1 Timothy 5:18.

In distinction from inspiration, divine teaching is the work of the Spirit enabling man to understand and appropriate personally this recorded revelation. "And 'he that is spiritual' — he in whom the Spirit abides to give understanding — discerns the meaning of the message and receives it as the testimony of God."[1]

Fourth, though borne along by the Spirit, the human authors of the books of the Bible did not always understand what they wrote. This is particularly noted in 1 Peter 1: 10-11: "Concerning which salvation the prophets sought and searched diligently, who prophesied of the grace that should come unto you: searching what time or what manner of time the Spirit of Christ which was in them did point unto, when it testified beforehand the sufferings of Christ, and the glories that should follow them."

The authors' lack of understanding of what they wrote in no way detracted from the certainty of their being used of God in inspiration.

In contrast to this is the fact that the Spirit's purpose in teaching is to make clear to the minds and hearts of God's children the truth which He has inspired.

If the Spirit's inspiring ministry is equated with His teaching ministry, inspiration tends to be degraded to a universally available mystical influence or provision of spiritual insight. This makes the human authors of Scripture differ from other Christians only in that "they were pioneers of conscience, and the consciousness of a divine commission made them prophets."[2] This is the view of Schleiermacher, who taught that the writers of Scripture were awakened in their religious consciousness and given religious intuitive feelings and insights. To confuse inspiration with the teaching of the Spirit debases Scripture or elevates the words of the saints to the level of the Scriptures. Gaussen illustrates how Jewish scholasticism and Roman Catholicism have been guilty of the latter.[3]

CONVICTION AND TEACHING

The ascension of Christ made possible the descent of the Spirit to "convict the world in respect of sin, and of righteousness, and of judgment" (Jn 16:8). This verse precedes the statement that the Spirit, "when he is come," will guide believers into all the truth (16:13). Thus, His coming provided for His carrying on two ministries: convicting the world and teaching believers. But what does the former of these mean? And how does it relate to His teaching of believers?

The word translated "convict" implies demonstrating by argument, refuting by proofs, *convincing* by means of unanswerable arguments.[4] The Greek courts of justice used the word in a legal sense to mean "convince of guilt."[5] It was not primarily the reprimanding of the guilty one, but rather the logical unanswerable demonstration of the fact of his guilt (making him conscious of his guilt). Thus the word did not convey so much the thought of bringing one to the point of *sorrow* for his sin as it did the idea of demonstrating the *guilt* of his sin.

This meaning is illustrated by the words of Christ in

John 8:46: "Which of you convicteth me of sin?" He did not mean, "Which of you can make Me feel sorry for sin?" Instead, He was asking, "Which of you can find proof that I am guilty?"

Sorrow of heart and, in turn, salvation may or may not follow from the convincing work of the Spirit. As the Holy Spirit *convinces* sinners regarding sin, righteousness, and judgment (Jn 16:8-11), some of them acknowledge their guilt, are sorrowful for sin, and turn to God for salvation, while others reject Christ.

In this ministry of convincing or demonstrating the guilt of sin, the Holy Spirit is, in a sense, "teaching" the unsaved. They are brought in contact with certain truths. They are "enlightened" regarding their sin, Christ's righteousness, and the judgment of sin. The Spirit places the truth in a clear light before sinners so that it may be seen and acknowledged as truth.

Some refer to this convincing work as an illuminating or enlightening of the unsaved, separate from the illuminating of the saved. Many consider it an "instructing" aspect of the work of the Spirit in common grace,[6] bestowed on every unregenerate person. This is referred to in John 1:9, "There was the true light . . . which lighteth every man that cometh into the world." Unbelievers are enlightened (or taught by demonstrable proof) concerning their sin, God's righteousness, and the work of the cross. The enlightenment may come through the preaching of the Word of God or by the direct, personal work of the Spirit on the mind and heart through the Word of God. In this enlightening, the Spirit is operating as Teacher, because He is illuminating with regard to certain truths requisite to an appropriation of salvation by faith in Jesus Christ. Chafer makes this summarizing statement:

> When the Spirit enlightens the Satan-blinded mind regarding sin, righteousness, and judgment, that otherwise blinded

mind is at once more than normally enabled to understand the three great foundational truths that sin has been judged, righteousness is available in and through Christ, and the condemning sin is failure to believe that which God now offers the sinner, namely, a perfect salvation in and through Christ the Saviour. No soul can be saved apart from this enlightenment, for no other power is sufficient to break the blindness which Satan has imposed on the minds of those who are lost.[7]

INDWELLING AND TEACHING

While the Spirit's indwelling of believers is not a teaching ministry as such, it is the basis for His teaching. Two verses in 1 John reveal the close relationship between the Spirit's indwelling and His teaching: "And ye have an anointing from the Holy One, and ye know all things. And as for you, the anointing which ye received of him abideth in you, and ye need not that any one teach you; but as his anointing teacheth you concerning all things, and is true, and is no lie, and even as it taught you, ye abide in him" (1 Jn 2: 20, 27).

Though the Holy Spirit is not explicitly referred to in these verses, He is certainly implied, as several factors indicate. For one thing, the figure of oil, which often symbolizes the Holy Spirit (Ps 45:7, 105:15; Is 61:1; Ac 10: 38), is used. Also, "the anointing" refers to the Holy Spirit, because the anointing comes from "the Holy One," who is Christ, according to Mark 1:24; John 6:69; and Acts 3: 14, 4:27. Christ promised to send the Spirit (Jn 14:26; 15:26; 16:7, 14). Second Corinthians 1:21-22, parallel to the passage in 1 John, clearly refers to the Holy Spirit. Also, the "anointing" is said in 1 John 2:27 to indwell believers, and this is a work of the Spirit frequently referred to in the Scriptures (Ro 8:9, 11; 1 Co 3:16, 6:19; Eph 2:22; 2 Ti 1:14; 1 Jn 3:24).

This anointing or indwelling of the Spirit is a once-for-all act that occurs at the moment of salvation. Because "the anointing . . . abideth in you" (1 Jn 2:27), it is a permanent, not a transient experience. It is the coming of the Spirit to take up His permanent residence in the hearts of believers. The anointing or indwelling of the Spirit makes it possible for Christians to be taught God's truth. "His anointing teacheth you." This does not mean, however, that every believer is necessarily fully taught by the Spirit.

> While the anointing with the Spirit makes possible His teaching ministry to the saint, it does not determine the fullness, richness, efficiency, or extent of that ministry. Every saint is anointed with the Spirit. But every saint is not the recipient of the best services of the Spirit in His teaching ministry.[8]

Perhaps the greatest problem in these two verses is the seeming exclusion of the need for human teachers, as indicated in the words, "and ye know all things" (1 Jn 2:20) and "ye need not that anyone teach you" (2:27). Do these verses mean that when the Holy Spirit indwells believers, He no longer uses human channels to impart His truth, and that believers have no need for further instruction because they possess all knowledge?

At least three interpretations have been given to the clause in 1 John 2:20, "and ye know all things." One involves a textual change to make the verse read "and ye all know." But the better Greek manuscripts do not favor this reading, and other internal evidence opposes it.*

Another interpretation supplies the word *needful* to the thought of the verse: "And ye know all needful things," that is, all things necessary for Christian living. But this seems to be inserting a thought not originally intended by the Holy Spirit.

---

*For example, in 1 John, the Greek verb here translated "know" always has an object.

A third view takes the verse as it reads, "And ye know all things," and understands it to mean the same thing intended by John when he wrote, "He shall teach you all things" (Jn 14:26) and, "He shall guide you into all the truth" (16:13). The meaning then, as Plummer puts it, is, "It is you (and not these antichristian Gnostics who claim it) that are in possession of the true knowledge, in virtue of the anointing of the Spirit of truth."[9] Gnostics in the early church claimed to know God's truth, but actually did not.

In 1 John 2:27 the clause, "And ye need not that any one teach you," also .needs careful consideration. The word *teach* is in the present tense, emphasizing continuous action. A helpful translation would be, "and ye have no need that anyone be teaching you."

This clause, too, has been explained in various ways. Kuyper takes it to mean that the church as a body needs no "outsider" to teach it, because it possesses all the treasures of wisdom and knowledge in Christ, its Head.[10]

A second view is that John is saying, "Ye need not be taught, only reminded" (in accord with the statement in Jn 14:26). Robertson holds this view.[11]

A third explanation refers it to man's *repetition* in teaching. Lenski paraphrases, "You are not a group of ignoramuses that need to be taught over and over by apostles and by Christian teachers."[12]

Representing a fourth view, Alford writes, "If that unction were abiding in them in all its fullness, they would have no need for His or any other teaching."[13]

A fifth, and perhaps the best, view understands the problem as one of ultimate source or authority. Wuest succinctly explains:

> It merely means that the saints are not at the mercy of these Gnostic teachers or at the mercy of any teachers, for that matter. No teacher, even a God-appointed one, is the only and ultimate source of the saint's instruction. He has the Holy Spirit and the Word.[14]

Simpson, writing on this passage, comments this way:

> It does not mean that we are not to receive the message
> of God from human lips; but it does mean we are not to
> receive any message as the word of man, but, even when
> we are taught by the ministers of Christ, we are to receive
> them as the messengers of God, to compare their word with
> God's Holy Word, and only to receive it as it is the voice of
> God speaking to our conscience in the Holy Ghost.[15]

Though God uses Christian teachers to communicate His
Word, ultimately learners are independent of man and must
be taught by God. Especially did the saints whom John
was addressing need this thought emphasized. They were in
danger of following the man-made teachings of Gnosticism,
rather than seeking to be taught by the Holy Spirit through
the Word.

Whatever the verse means, it clearly does *not* mean that
the Spirit supersedes all necessity for instruction. First John
2:1, 24, indicate that even John himself was teaching his
readers through his writing the epistle!

It is important not to overlook the second half of 1 John
2:27: "But as his anointing teacheth you concerning all
things, and is true, and is no lie, and even as it taught you,
ye abide [or, *abide ye*] in him." Though indwelt by the
blessed Holy Spirit, Christians are capable of receiving the
teaching ministry of the Spirit only as they "abide in him."

ILLUMINATION AND TEACHING

The illuminating work of the Holy Spirit is frequently referred to in Scripture. The Greek word for *enlighten* means
"to give light, shine"; "to . . . light up, illumine"; and "to
enlighten spiritually, imbue with saving knowledge."[16] The
third classification relates this work of the Spirit to that of
teaching or bestowing knowledge. The figure is that of the
light of knowledge penetrating and dispelling the darkness

of ignorance. The following verses show how illumination is related to knowledge: "Seeing it is God, that said, Light shall shine out of darkness, who shined in our hearts, to give the light of the knowledge of the glory of God in the face of Jesus Christ" (2 Co 4:6).

"That the God of our Lord Jesus Christ, the Father of glory, may give unto you a spirit of wisdom and revelation in the knowledge of him; having the eyes of your heart enlightened, that ye may know what is the hope of his calling, what the riches of the glory of his inheritance in the saints" (Eph 1:17-18).

Unbelievers are spoken of as "having the understanding darkened" (Eph 4:18, KJV). This emphasizes the need for illumination. God has given to men general and special revelation, but sin has blinded them to it. Thus they cannot receive God's external, objective revelation. God's Word is not in any way defective or insufficient. The fault lies with man. It is as though a blind man were facing the sun. The fact that he cannot see the light is not the fault of the sun; the deficiency lies with him.

Non-Christians are spiritually blind. Their hearts are hardened, they are insensitive to God, they are blinded to God's truth. The Holy Spirit must open the eyes of their minds and hearts and give them spiritual enlightenment or illumination.

> The Word of God is like the sun shining on all to whom it is preached; but without any benefit to the blind. But in this respect we are all blind by nature, therefore it cannot penetrate into our minds, unless this internal teacher, the Spirit, makes way for it by His illumination.[17]

There is a sense in which all non-Christians are illuminated (Jn 1:9). But not all are the "sons of light" (Jn 12:36). The special work of God's Spirit by which He moves non-Christians to believe the revealed truth of salvation and accept Christ as Saviour is His work of regeneration.

But saints, too, are in need of illumination, as evidenced by the psalmist's cry, "Open thou mine eyes, that I may behold wondrous things out of thy law" (Ps 119:18). Paul prayed that the Ephesians, who were believers, may have the eyes of their hearts enlightened (Eph 1:17-18). As Christ talked with the Emmaus disciples, He "opened . . . their mind, that they might understand the scriptures" (Lk 24:45).

From these facts, then, it is clear that illumination is that supernatural work of the Spirit whereby He enables man to apprehend the already revealed truth of God. But is this a work of the Spirit on the mind only? Does illumination imply that some believers are able to penetrate Scripture to grasp new truths or "deep" meanings that others cannot understand? Does it imply that new mental faculties are endowed by the Spirit on some believers, so that they can see underlying truths not readily ascertainable from the text?

In answer to these penetrating questions some things must be said:

First, the illumination of the Spirit always relates to the Word of God, the Bible. This is clear from verses such as Psalm 119:18, 130; John 14:26; and Revelation 22:18. No new truth is revealed in illumination. The Bible is God's complete written revelation, beyond which the Spirit of God reveals no new truths. To give new truths to non-Christians would be as useless as trying to make a blind man see by putting two suns in the sky.[18] He does not need added content or knowledge, but the opening of the eyes of his heart so he can see the revelation already given.

Second, illumination is more appropriately defined as the work of the Spirit on the mind *and heart* of man, enabling him to apprehend the truth of God already revealed. Ephesians 1:18 speaks of the "eyes of your *heart*" being enlightened (the KJV wrongly translates "heart" as "understanding"). Lydia's *heart* was opened (Ac 16:14). The mind and heart together comprise what Kuyper calls the "spiritual consciousness."[19] Spiritual truths demand the response of the affections and will, as well as the understanding.

Third, illumination involves not simply the perception but also the *reception* of truth. It is not so much a mental apprehension of "deep" truths as it is a personal welcoming and *appropriation* of truths understood. To receive God's truths fully, one must first understand them and then appropriate them. Bromiley expresses this fact when he says that the Holy Spirit, who has given the Word of God, seeks to "open the eyes of the readers to perceive its truth and receive its light."[20] Obviously unsaved men can mentally grasp something of the objective data of the Bible. Many unbelievers have mentally grasped many of the historical facts presented in the Word of God. Some have even followed the logic of certain portions of the Bible. They have mentally grasped certain objective biblical facts — that certain Bible personalities performed certain tasks, said certain words, went to certain geographical locations, argued with certain points of logic, and so on — *yet* they do not know the God of the Scriptures. Even with determined application and research on a high scholarly level, they are unable to arrive at the true divine sense of the Scriptures.[21] The Spirit's illuminating of Christians, then, must include something more than mental apprehension of the Bible of which non-Christians are capable.

Though the unsaved may mentally observe objective data of the Bible, it remains foolishness to them (1 Co 1:18, 2:14). Though perhaps able to follow the logic of Paul's reasoning in his epistles, unbelievers do not "take to heart" the truth involved. The grammar of John 3:16 may be clear to natural men, but this does not mean that they receive to their hearts the truth of the verse. Sinful men do not welcome God's truth, because it strikes at the very core of their sinfulness.

Only the saved are able to *welcome* God's truth. When Paul states in 1 Corinthians 2:14 that "the natural man receiveth not the things of the Spirit of God," he does not mean that the natural man is totally incapable of apprehending any of the grammatical data of the Bible. Rather, Paul means that the unsaved man does not welcome its truth! The Greek word translated "receive" means "welcome." The verse does not mean that the natural man, who is devoid of the Holy Spirit, cannot *understand* mentally what the Bible is saying; instead it means that he cannot *welcome* its message of redemption to his own heart.[22]

The statement in 1 Corinthians 2:14 that the things of the Spirit of God are "foolishness unto him" would indicate that the natural man had some understanding of what the Bible says. Otherwise, if nothing were communicated to the unsaved man, how could he judge such a communication to be foolish?

"But," one may argue, "this verse also states that the unsaved man cannot even *know* the things of the Spirit. Does not this argue *against* the point being made that the unsaved can be cognizant of Bible facts?" No, because the Greek word that is used means *know by experience.* An unbeliever does not know God's truth experientially. He may discern portions of it mentally, but he does not experience it personally.

In illumination the Holy Spirit's work is not only to show what the Bible means, but also to persuade Christians of its truth. Illumination is the Spirit's work, enabling Christians to discern the meaning of the message and to welcome and receive it as from God. Hodge states that obedience in the believer's life is the inevitable result of the illuminating work of the Spirit.[24]

This concept of illumination is also verified by the words of Christ to the unbelieving Pharisees. He did not denounce them for not understanding the facts of the truth; they understood the "letter of the law" better than perhaps any other people in their day. He denounced them, however, for not appropriating the truth as God's truth. Paul did not rebuke the carnal Corinthians for failing to have a mental grasp of the facts of the Bible, but for not receiving to their hearts what they understood in their minds. For this reason, he said, "Ye were not yet able to bear it; nay, not even now are ye able; for ye are yet carnal" (1 Co 3:2-3). In illumination the Spirit helps believers understand the implications and values of God's truth and welcome it with a view to personal heartfelt appropriation. Because the Bible is more than a human book, it can be rightly apprehended only by those who are given the divine enablement of the Holy Spirit. Karl Barth wrongly equates this ministry of the Spirit with His ministry of revelation. Mueller writes that "Barth regards only that as the Word of God which the Spirit impresses upon the individual human mind as such, or as we may say, the Bible is God's Word only so far as God spoke through it. If God does not speak through the Scriptures, they are not God's Word but merely man's word."[24] Barth's view denies the objectivity of divine truth and rejects the Scriptures as infallibly authoritative. This matter will be discussed more fully in Part 3. Without this ministry of the Spirit, the Bible remains to man a spiritual enigma.

It is clear from these facts that illumination is more than some flash of mental insight or intuition. Miller espouses a low view of illumination:

> The Holy Spirit provides the gift of *illumination.* This may be the inner light . . . , the warmth of heart . . . , the intuition granted to a scientist, the moment of truth which comes to all of us when we see clearly what the truth is for us. We ascribe this gift to the Holy Spirit because we can never predict the moment when the light will come down.[25]

How does illumination relate to the teaching work of the Spirit? Some think His teaching and illuminating work are identical. Others prefer to think of the teaching as broader, including both revelation and illumination.† The Spirit's work of revelation (giving an objective body of truth, the Bible) was completed when the last words of the Bible were inspired. But He now works on the outer Word, to make it inner in the lives of believers.

In teaching, the Holy Spirit operates on (or activates) both the written Word and pupils: one He animates and the other He illuminates. It is in this way that He communicates, or teaches, God's truth. Teaching, then, is the broader term and includes the revealing and animating of the Word, along with the illuminating of the hearts and minds of believers.

From this study of the biblical doctrine of the Holy Spirit as Teacher, it is seen that teaching is no minor phase of the Spirit's work. As the Spirit of truth, He gives understanding, wisdom, counsel, and knowledge; He imparts and appropriates truth; He teaches and guides believers into all God's revelation; He reminds of Christ's teachings; He announces things that are coming; and He reveals the truth of God to man. He convinces sinners of their guilt; He anoints or indwells believers so that they need not rely on inadequate sources for learning God's truth; and He illumines the minds and hearts of believers to enable them to welcome and appropriate God's Word.

The Holy Spirit's ministry of teaching is infallible, personal, centered on Christ, and related to the Word of God. May God enable every believer to be receptive to this one whom the Father has sent in Christ's stead.

---

†In a sense, illumination is revelation of a sort. But strictly speaking, biblical revelation is the communication of God's truth in written form, while illumination is the communication of the *meaning* of the truth. However, the Spirit in illumination is not creating *new* truths. He *has* communicated the truth, once for all recorded infallibly in the Bible. Rather than giving new truths, He guides into truth already revealed. Of course, to the believer being illumined, the truths may be new, for he has never before known them. Only in this sense is illumination an aspect of revelation.

Part 2

TEACHERS AND THE TEACHER

Because the Holy Spirit is the Teacher of God's truth, what part do human teachers have in Christian teaching?

Does the teaching ministry of the Holy Spirit eliminate the need for human teachers? Does the work of teachers in Christian education imply that the Spirit is not sufficient to teach truths and change lives?

Is Christian education merely a human process, leaving no room for the Holy Spirit? Are Christian teachers left to their own human resources? Is the Holy Spirit not in need of human teachers, since His work is divine?

If human teachers and the Spirit are to work together, what is the distinct functioning of each? What does God do in teaching that teachers cannot do? What are teachers expected to do, and for what does God hold them responsible? How can the divine and human cooperate in their teaching responsibilities?

Whenever God has employed human instruments to accomplish His purposes, man has been puzzled to know, and often has misunderstood, how and why God works in such fashion. The human mind wonders, for instance, how God could have employed fallible human authors to compose an infallible Book. The human mind has difficulty comprehending how God could have employed a fallible human being — a virgin — to give birth to an infallible person, the incarnate Christ. So it is in teaching. How does God employ human teachers in a divine process to change lives?

4

False Views on the Divine and Human Teachers

LET US CAREFULLY CONSIDER several false views regarding the relationship of the Holy Spirit to human teachers.

THE HOLY SPIRIT EXCLUDES HUMAN TEACHERS

Mystic subjectivists believe that because the Holy Spirit illuminates believers directly, human teachers are unnecessary. This view implies that God's teaching is obstructed, not helped, by human teachers. This viewpoint obviously tends to lead to the conclusion that Christians do not need to study, go to school, or sit under teachers, because the Holy Spirit is their Teacher.

The post-Reformation Pietist movement, which stressed the direct teaching work of the Spirit intuitively on the soul, led to an overt disdain toward study and education.[1] According to this view, methods of teaching, educational materials, and programs are efforts of the flesh and are fallible, carnal, and deficient. Any effort of human beings to transmit God's living truth only contaminates and trespasses on the priority of the Holy Spirit.

Sometimes Bible-believing Christians fall prey to this kind of fallacious thinking, supposing that education is the enemy of spirituality.

Some people adhere to this concept in order to shade their own deficiencies in learning ability or in educational training. Others maintain such a view as an indirect means of calling attention to their own supposedly superior spiritual state, which enables learning to stem directly from the Spirit. Others who maintain this view do so because of an overly cautious concern that Christianity be guarded against the extremes of intellectualism, dead orthodoxy, or progressive education.

The following facts argue against this view:

First, even in biblical times, God used human teachers to impart His truth to others. Christ's Great Commission included the command to teach (Mt 28:19-20). The early church leaders were engaged in a ministry of teaching and preaching (Ac 5:42, 15:35, 18:11, 28:31). Apollos taught others the things of the Lord (Ac 18:25), and Timothy was commanded "to teach others" (2 Ti 2:2).

Second, the fact that God has given men the gift of teaching and has given such gifted men to the church is evidence that He uses human instruments to communicate His truth (Ro 12:6-7; 1 Co 12:28; Eph 4:11).

Third, the writer of the book of Hebrews tells his readers that they should be teaching others (Heb 5:12).

Therefore, it is unscriptural to suppose that the work of God's Spirit necessarily excludes His working through Christian teachers to lead others to the truth of God's Word.*

---

*Though it is true that the Spirit can and does often teach believers directly, apart from human teachers, this possibility and its functioning is not the point under discussion. The issue is not *can* God work alone, but *does* He? "God can work in sovereign grace independent of us, though He seldom chooses to do so" (Lois E. LeBar, *Education That Is Christian*, p. 230).

THE HOLY SPIRIT SUBSTITUTES FOR HUMAN EFFORT

The erroneous concept that the Holy Spirit substitutes for human effort is similar to the one above; but it is different in that the other view excludes altogether the necessity of teachers, whereas this view excludes only the need for preparation, study, or effort on the part of teachers. Edge thus describes adherents of this view:

> There are those teachers who seem to feel that because they are teaching the Bible they do not have to know or follow proved educational principles. They do not want to be bothered with these "new-fangled" ideas. Their attitude, simply stated, is "I just teach the Bible and let the chips fall where they may."[2]

Some of those who have this attitude maintain that little or no training or preparation is needed, because, in the final analysis, the results in teaching come from the Holy Spirit.

This viewpoint is faulty for three reasons:

First, it is based on a wrong concept of teaching. In good teaching, the teacher is more than a "presenter" of truth; he is concerned about doing all in his power to develop lives, to lead pupils to Christlike living — all through the Holy Spirit. As Benson has suggested, "the *object* of our teaching is to make something happen in the life of our pupil."[3] Only the teacher who is well prepared can do the most efficient task, while at the same time relying on the Holy Spirit to work *through* him in the lives of his students. Benson argues pointedly in this connection with these words:

> We believe and insist upon Spirit-filled teachers, but can we hope that the Holy Spirit will honor unnecessary and unwarranted ignorance? As teachers, we are only instruments upon which the Holy Spirit must play, but surely it will make a difference whether the instrument is in tune or not. . . . If our teachers are to be tuned instruments for God's use, ought they not to be prepared? We want Spirit-

filled teachers, but the Holy Spirit is not honored by our ignorance or by our indolence.[4]

Second, those who hold this view fail to see that teaching is a divine-human process. The teacher and the Spirit are involved together in the teaching process. To the extent that the teacher is inefficient, the process becomes ineffective and learning is hampered. Though the Spirit may teach pupils in spite of the inadequacies of the teacher, more learning can take place when the teacher is prepared, is depending on the Holy Spirit, and is adjusted personally to his Teammate, the Holy Spirit. "Surely the Lord can use to better advantage teachers who are thoroughly equipped for their work than those who are not."[5]

Third, this viewpoint, rather than magnifying the Bible and emphasizing the power of the Holy Spirit, borders on presuming on God "because it seeks to make God do what He is not supposed to do."[6]

The question may be asked, Is it possible, then, for Christian teachers to depend too much on the Holy Spirit? The answer is an unquestionable no, if Christian teachers depend on the Spirit for spiritual enablement, for guidance as they prepare to teach, for illumination of their minds and hearts, for spiritual direction. The answer may be yes, if the teachers are supposedly depending on the Spirit to the exclusion of preparing their own hearts and minds for the particular class sessions for which they are responsible. A teacher should not ask or expect God to do for him that for which God holds him responsible.

Paul's statement in 1 Corinthians 3:6 conclusively argues for the fact that human effort is coupled with, not to be substituted by, the divine working of God Himself: "I planted, Apollos watered; but God gave the increase." Christian teachers are responsible to find God's ways of working and work with Him, and should not try to exploit the Holy

Spirit's ministry as an excuse for their own weakness, laziness, or ignorance.

THE HOLY SPIRIT ADDS A SPIRITUAL
FOOTNOTE TO TEACHING

Another subtle, often misunderstood false concept about how the Holy Spirit teaches is that the Holy Spirit adds a "footnote" or a blessing to whatever is taught. If teachers suppose that Christian teaching is no different from secular teaching, except that they can ask God to bless their efforts, they fail to understand the way in which the Spirit operates in true Christian teaching. Teaching does not suddenly become Christian when a spiritual footnote is added to that which the teacher imparts. Rather, biblical truth must be interwoven by the Spirit into the very fabric of teaching, if it is to be considered Christian education.

As the Holy Spirit teaches, He does more than add a halo or appendix to what has been taught. His ministry is more than a mere taking over where teachers leave off. To think of the teaching of the Spirit as an annex to the work of human teachers is to overlook the fact that the Spirit teaches pupils before and during classroom situations, as well as afterward. Such thinking fails to see that the divine Teacher and human teachers are to work together as a team, simultaneously. When God is educating, the human teacher and the pupils are involved together in the teaching-learning process, and at the same time the Spirit is working within the teacher, on the Word of God, and within the pupils.

THE HOLY SPIRIT IS TOTALLY UNNECESSARY

This view that the Holy Spirit is unnecessary, is an extreme opposite of the first two views and is held by some who are involved in the task of religious teaching. Those who appreciate the importance of educational theory and practice, of methods and materials, of curriculum and equipment, sometimes tend to overlook the supernatural element so essential to Christian education.

They feel that if they are given the right set of methods, the correct combination of learning situations, the proper materials and equipment, and the ideal teaching-learning patterns, Christian learning and growth will naturally follow. This view is frequently held by liberal religious educators.

A neglect of the Spirit's ministry may also stem from the idea that such a consideration of the Holy Spirit is an attempt to understand the inscrutable workings of God. But, as LeBar explains, "Not that we should try to unscrew the inscrutable, but those things which God has revealed belong to us and to our children"[7] (Deu 29:29). Others shy from viewing the Spirit of God essential in Christian teaching because of an unwarranted fear that emotional subjectivism may find its way into education. Pride in one's self-accomplishments in teaching may be still another reason why some disregard the necessity of the Spirit.

The following factors argue against such a view:

First, to think of the Spirit as unnecessary is to depend on the futile workings of the flesh. If a person attempts to teach God's truths in his own power, he is wasting his time and energy in sterile unfruitfulness.

Second, this view tends to consider educational methods and procedures as ends in themselves. Methods are inherent in all that educators do, but it is wrong to be so taken up by the mechanics of Christian education that the essential dynamics of the workings of God's Spirit are overlooked. Some Christian teachers have faithfully followed sound educational principles and used excellent teaching techniques but have still been unsuccessful in teaching, because they have not been guided and empowered by the Holy Spirit.

Third, this concept fails to take into consideration the ultimate spiritual goals of Christian education. It overlooks the fact that God is the Teacher, and that pupils have needs that are far more than intellectual. Christian education seeks to do more than impart knowledge of truth to the head; it seeks to transform the life, by means of the Holy Spirit and the Word. Believers should desire the Word of God so that they "may grow [not merely know] thereby" (1 Pe 2:2). Hence, the absolutely indispensable factor in Christian teaching is the inner working of God's Spirit in the lives of pupils, through His holy Word.

5

What Is the Gift of Teaching?

MUCH CONFUSION and ignorance regarding spiritual gifts (and particularly the gift of teaching) has prevailed among Christians. Proper understanding of the spiritual gift of teaching will enable believers to perceive more accurately how the divine and human teachers should function together.

THE NATURE OF SPIRITUAL GIFTS

Before considering the specific gift of teaching, certain general facts relating to gifts may be considered.

First, it is clear from Scripture that every believer has some gift. "To *each* one is given the manifestation of the Spirit to profit withal" (1 Co 12:7), and "all these worketh the one and the same Spirit, dividing to *each* one severally even as he will" (1 Co 12:11). Gifts are given "according as God hath dealt to *each* man a measure of faith" (Ro 12:3) and should be exercised "according as *each* hath received a gift" (1 Pe 4:10). "Unto *each* one of us was the grace given according to the measure of the gift of Christ" (Eph 4:7).

In Scripture, spiritual gifts are often associated with the fact that believers are members of the body of Christ. Because each Christian is a member of Christ's body, he has

66

been given a spiritual gift, however small or insignificant it may seem to be, to exercise in the body. "We, who are many, are one body in Christ, and severally members one of another" (Ro 12:5). Christians are in "the body of Christ, and severally members thereof" (1 Co 12:27), and Christ "gave gifts unto men" (Eph 4:8) "unto the building up of the body of Christ" (4:12). Each believer has a function in the body of Christ by virtue of a spiritual gift which he is to exercise.

Second, there is great diversity, and yet unity, among the gifts. "Now there are diversities [varieties] of gifts, but the same Spirit. And there are diversities of ministrations [varieties of service], and the same Lord" (1 Co 12:4-5). The gifts differ according to the grace given to believers (Ro 12:6). The lists of gifts (in Ro 12:6-8; 1 Co 12:4-11, 28-30; and Eph 4:7-12) specify a great richness in the variety and diversity of gifts. Walvoord states that there are at least 16 spiritual gifts enumerated in the New Testament.[1]

Yet, in this rich diversification there is uniformity and harmony, as indicated by the six occurrences of the word *same* in 1 Corinthians 12:4-11. "The one aim of these gifts is to minister to the unity of the Body, for unity is wrought through diversity"[2] (Eph 4:13, 16). Just as there are many parts to one physical body, so there are many members with varied gifts in the one body of Christ (1 Co 12:18-20; Eph 4:4).

Third, spiritual gifts are of divine origin and sovereignly bestowed by God. Each member is placed in the body with a particular gift or gifts, according to God's sovereign will. God divides "to each one severally even as *he* will" (1 Co 12:11), and *"God* set the members each one of them in the body, even as it pleased *him"* (12:18). *"God* hath dealt to every man a measure of faith" (Ro 12:3). This fact should cause believers not to covet jealously those gifts that other believers possess. An attitude of humility should accompany the exercise of spiritual gifts, for they are all undeserved.

> Because their bestowal is sovereign, it follows that it is not a question of spirituality. A Christian unyielded to the Lord may possess great spiritual value, while one yielded may have relatively minor spiritual abilities. . . . It remains true, of course, that proper adjustment in the spiritual life of the believer is essential to proper exercise of his gifts, but spirituality does not bring spiritual gifts.[3]

God bestows gifts on believers because of His sovereign grace. It is interesting that the word for spiritual gifts is derived from the word for grace.

Fourth, some gifts are permanent, while others were temporary, having been exercised only in the apostolic period. The gifts possessed by some believers in the church today are the gift of teaching, the gift of evangelism, the gift of pastoring, the gift of exhorting, the gift of giving, the gift of showing mercy, the gift of helping, the gift of administering, the gift of discerning spirits, and the gift of faith. Among the temporary gifts are apostleship, prophecy, performing miracles, healing, tongues, and interpreting tongues. Walvoord cogently demonstrates the temporary nature of these latter gifts in his book on the Holy Spirit.[4]

Fifth, spiritual gifts are given so that the body of Christ may be edified. Each gift is to be exercised for the profit and benefit of others. "But to each one is given the manifestation of the Spirit to profit withal" (1 Co 12:7). Gifts were given "for the perfecting of the saints, unto the work of ministering, unto the building up of the body of Christ" (Eph 4:12).

Paul is very anxious that spiritual gifts be used to *edification* (1 Co 14:4-5, 12, 26). Spiritual gifts are given not for the outward displaying of individual abilities, but for the practical purpose of equipping the saints for ministering to the body of Christ. "Unity and utility define the aim of all the gifts and prescribe their legitimate exercise."[5]

Spiritual gifts, then, are divinely bestowed endowments of

grace empowering believers to minister to the edifying of the church. They are related to the Holy Spirit in that they are each a "manifestation of the Spirit" (1 Co 12:7).

THE NATURE OF THE GIFT OF TEACHING

The gift of teaching is of primary importance in the ministry of Christian education in the local church. It is one of the major gifts, for it is mentioned specifically in each of the three lists of gifts in the New Testament (Ro 12:7-8; 1 Co 12:28; Eph 4:11). Its importance is also highlighted by the fact that it is frequently mentioned along with the apostolic gift of prophecy (Ac 13:1; Ro 12:6-7; 1 Co 12: 28-29; Eph 4:11). Since the temporary gifts of apostleship and prophecy were necessary only in the transitional phase of the apostolic period, the gift of teaching may be considered one of the first in the rank of permanent gifts for today (1 Co 12:28). (Not that some gifts are more essential than others [1 Co 12:14-18], but some appear to be more prominent than others [14:24].)

Teaching was also closely associated with preaching (Ac 5:42; 1 Ti 2:7; 2 Ti 1:11), and is closely linked with the gift of pastoring. In Ephesians 4:11 the Greek words for "pastors" and "teachers" are closely linked. Also, the word translated "some," occuring before the word "pastors," is omitted before the word "teachers." This implies that one cannot be a true pastor without also being a teacher. One way in which a pastor or shepherd cares for his flock is by teaching them. The pastor-teacher compares to the "teaching priest" of the Old Testament (2 Ch 15:3).

The teaching gift is of primary importance in the edifying of the church. Since gifts are given for ministering to the body of Christ, it is clear that those who are most effective in this spiritual task of edification are those who possess and are cultivating the gift of teaching. Many seek to be teachers but are not met with any degree of spiritual success in their efforts because they are without the teaching gift. The spiritually minded Christian educator will recognize that many local church workers in positions of teaching do not possess the gift of teaching.

But what is the gift of teaching? Like other spiritual gifts, it is a supernatural ability. The gift of teaching is a supernatural, Spirit-endowed ability to expound (explain and apply) the truth of God. Teaching differs from exhortation in that the latter is the ability to persuade and encourage others in the active realization of the will of God, whereas teaching is the gift of systematic instruction and application in the doctrines (or teachings) of God's truths.[6] Though all believers in fellowship with the Holy Spirit are taught by Him, not all believers have the ability to teach others as effectively as those who have the teaching gift. A Christian teacher with the gift of teaching does not necessarily know more about the Word of God than others, but that gift does enable him to impart more effectively that which he does know.

The relationship between the spiritual gift of teaching and the natural ability for teaching is an important aspect of this subject. Spiritual gifts clearly pertain to the spiritual birth of a believer rather than to his natural birth. This is clear for several reasons: (1) Obviously, the Scriptures never speak of non-Christians possessing spiritual gifts. (2) Spiritual gifts are more than manifestations of human ability because they are called "gifts." (3) They are given for edifying the body of Christ, and therefore are related to the believer's new nature. (4) Spiritual gifts are called manifestations of the Spirit (1 Co 12:7).

Does this mean, then, that all spiritual gifts are of a vividly supernatural nature? Does an individual who before salvation had no ability or interests in, say, teaching, suddenly at salvation possess the gift of teaching? Or is it possible that believers who are given the gift of teaching are often those who have had some natural teaching ability before they were saved? Though the Bible does not answer these questions explicitly, scriptural illustrations seem to shed some light on this problem.

Aholiab, for instance, was by natural ability "an engraver, and a skilful workman, and an embroiderer" (Ex 38:23). But for working on the tabernacle, God filled him (and Bezaleel and other wisehearted men) with the Spirit of God "in wisdom, and in understanding, and in knowledge, and in all manner of workmanship" (31:3; cf. 35: 30-35) "for the service of the sanctuary" (36:1).

The "wisehearted" tailors who made Aaron's garments were naturally skilled in that craft, but in addition to their natural ability, God filled them with the Spirit of wisdom (28:3).

Before Paul was saved, he had been trained in the schools of his day. His natural abilities, along with his training, made him a capable teacher, orator, leader, and administrator. It is interesting that after salvation his spiritual gifts were in line with these natural gifts (1 Ti 2:7). Even today many people with evident talents in a certain sphere have been used of God mightily in that same sphere after salvation. For example, persons gifted in administering before salvation, often find that they can best minister to the upbuilding of the church by exercising the spiritual gift of administering. Thus it is clear that at least some spiritual gifts have a basis in natural talent. But this in no way minimizes the element of sovereign bestowal. It is still a work of God to enable believers to use their natural abilities to the glory of God in a spiritual sphere.

Since spiritual gifts are sometimes (if not often) in accord with natural gifts, then what is the difference between a natural ability before salvation, and the same ability after salvation? Many Bible commentators agree that the difference lies in a spiritual enhancing or strengthening of the natural ability. Lenski makes this comment: "Some of these gifts have a natural basis in natural talents and abilities.

The Spirit sanctifies and augments these talents for His high and blessed purpose."[7]

Dewar states that natural abilities are greatly enriched when they are consecrated, whereas other gifts "are clearly supernatural and in no way are they dependent upon natural talents."[8]

Those spiritual gifts, then, which are in accord with pre-conversion natural abilities, are an enhancing of those natural gifts, a channeling of those abilities into spiritual spheres of ministry, and involve a "special quickening to accomplish the task."[9] And all three factors are necessarily involved: an enhancing, a channeling, and a quickening. In keeping with this viewpoint, there seems to be no apparent reason why certain characteristics common to both a natural and a spiritual ability may not be evident in the individual before salvation. The fact that spiritual gifts are bestowed at the time of salvation does not outrule the fact that God may be preparing a person before salvation along certain lines, in keeping with spiritual gifts, which God plans for him to possess and exercise after salvation. This may often be true of the gift of teaching. Believers who possess the teaching gift may often be those whom God has been preparing, before their salvation, in areas related to a teaching ministry. But this is not *always* the case. "It may be frequently observed that individuals with little natural talent are often used mightily of God when those with great natural talent, though saved, are never similarly used."[10]

Regardless of what is said about this difficult problem of the relationship between spiritual gifts and natural abilities, there can be no question about the divine origin and providential appointment of spiritual gifts. Whether or not the spiritual gift of teaching is given in accord with the natural ability of teaching, it is still true that this gift has its origin in God and consists of a supernatural divine enablement to expound and impart the Word of God to others.

Is the gift of teaching essential for teaching secular subjects, or is it needed only by those teaching the Bible? Cannot regenerate teachers successfully teach subjects such as biology, music, or mathematics without the spiritual gift of teaching?

Offhand it would appear that this gift would be needed for teaching only biblical subjects. However, a closer consideration of the problem and the issues involved indicates otherwise. For one thing, Scripture does not warrant a sharp line of demarcation between "secular" truth and "spiritual" truth. As Gaebelein has well expounded, "all truth is God's truth."[11]

Of course, revealed truth as recorded in the Bible is of higher importance than "natural" truth. But the latter is within the framework of God's truth, and needs to be taught as such. From this standpoint, it would appear that Christian teachers must be just as divinely enabled for teaching history or music as for teaching the Bible — provided they are interested in teaching these truths from a Christian frame of reference. In fact, the difficult task of integrating some so-called secular subjects into a Christian framework may demand even more divine ability than the task of expounding the Bible.

Spiritual gifts are given to persons, not to occasions. Believers who have received the spiritual gift of teaching are to exercise it, not merely on some teaching occasions but in teaching any truth. Christian teachers should utilize every teaching opportunity to orient students in their study of the "secular" to a Christian world view. They should relate the principles of God's Word and Christianity to every subject they teach — and to do this, they must possess and exercise the spiritual gift of teaching. To teach biology from a Christian perspective is to teach, in a sense, spiritual (or God's) truth. Christian teachers must be divinely enabled by God's Spirit to expound to others God's truth — whether "secular" or spiritual.

The call, then, is for a wholly Christian world view on the part of our education. We must recognize, for example, that we need teachers who see their subjects, whether scientific, historical, mathematical, literary, or artistic, as included within the pattern of God's truth. It is one thing to take for ourselves the premise that all truth is God's truth. It is another thing to build upon this premise an effective educational practice that shows the student the unity of truth and that brings alive in his heart and mind the grand concept of a Christ who "is the image of the invisible God," by whom "all things were created," who "is before all things," and by whom "all things consist," or hold together.[12]

The Function of the Gift of Teaching

How is the gift of teaching discovered? How should it be developed and exercised? And what does all this imply?

It is one thing to be given a spiritual gift, but it is another thing to know what that gift is. All believers possess at least one spiritual gift, but many are not aware of what their gift or gifts may be. Spiritual gifts bestowed by God on believers are permanent possessions. Those gifts do not come and go. The exercise or use of the gifts may be intermittent, but the possession of them is permanent.

The duty of each believer, in reference to spiritual gifts, is to discover what his gift is and then to develop and exercise it to the glory of God.

In a sense *all* believers are teachers. Believers are exhorted to teach and admonish one another (Col 3:16). "Bishops" and "the Lord's servants" must be "apt to teach" (1 Ti 3: 2; 2 Ti 2:24). Timothy was told by Paul to commit to faithful men the things he had heard from Paul, so that they in turn may "be able to teach others also" (2 Ti 2:2). On the other hand, the special gift of teaching is bestowed only on some believers.

It is the duty of every believer to discover what his gift may be. It is one thing to have the gift of teaching, but it is another to have the gift of teaching and know it. It is conceivable that some believers possess the gift of teaching but are totally unaware of the fact. Having never exercised the gift, they may not be aware of this latent spiritually endowed ability. Either they have not been instructed about the matter of spiritual gifts, or they are out of fellowship with the Lord and are thus incapable of receiving and appropriating spiritual truth.

How, then, may one determine if he has the gift of teaching? Several guideposts may be mentioned. As noted before, sometimes this gift is given in accord with the natural ability of teaching. Therefore, if a person were gifted as a teacher before he was saved, he should consider whether this may be his spiritual gift for edifying Christ's body. It may be or may not be.

Another means of determining whether one has the gift of teaching is to minister in several capacities in the local church and elsewhere. If one possesses the gift of teaching, either he or others or both may discover his latent ability, as he ministers in a teaching capacity.

Another token by which this gift may be determined is the evident blessing of God on one's teaching. Often, spiritual results and blessings evidenced in one's ministry are a divine token that the believer has struck on that which God has intended as his prescribed ministry to the body of Christ. All this applies to laymen as well as to Christians in "full-time" Christian teaching capacities. Obviously, a Christian cannot accurately ascertain God's intentions for him in this direction unless he is in the center of God's will, filled by the Spirit.

To discover a spiritual gift is only the first step toward its effective utilization. As a believer lives in God's will, he is then in the proper spiritual condition for developing his gift of teaching. The exhortation to develop and increase the effectiveness of one's gift is stated at least three times in the Bible. Twice Paul addresses Timothy regarding his spiritual

gift. (Whether Timothy had the gift of teaching is not fully
clear in Scripture.) "Neglect not the gift that is in thee. . . .
Be diligent in these things" (1 Ti 4:14-15). "I put thee in
remembrance that thou stir up the gift of God which is in
thee" (2 Ti 1:6). The Greek word translated "stir up"
means "to kindle into flame." Timothy was to exercise his
gift in the sense of fanning it into a flame. He was to kindle
or rouse to the utmost his latent gift. He was to exercise it,
not neglect it by letting it lie unused.

The exercising of spiritual gifts is to be done as an act of
stewardship. "According as each hath received a gift, ministering it among yourselves, as good stewards of the mani-
fold grace of God" (1 Pe 4:10). A spiritual gift is an entrustment, as well as an enablement and endowment. If a
Christian has the teaching gift, he is responsible to care for
it as a steward would his master's household. "However rich
the gifts which God has bestowed upon us, they do not
grow of their own accord, but need to be cultivated by our
own personal care."[13]

Various means by which one may develop his gift of
teaching are: observing others who have the gift, getting
training and schooling in how to teach, and gaining teaching experience. As a good steward of that which God has
sovereignly bestowed, a Christian teacher will be anxious to
do all he can to improve and make the best use of his gift.

Nothing is basically wrong or unspiritual in getting training and schooling to improve one's gift of teaching. Anything that can be done to better the use of one's gifts to the
glory of Christ and the edification of the church should be
undertaken and is in harmony with the exhortation in 1 Peter
4:10 to be "good stewards."

The objection may be raised, "How can a teacher improve
on that which God has done or given? When God imparts
the gift of teaching, it is imparted perfectly. At that moment,
a teacher is as good a teacher as he will ever be. To try to
improve what God has done is to mix mundane and fleshly

efforts with a spiritual gift." This objection may be answered in three ways:

First, experience shows that this objection is without basis. When a person begins to teach as, say, a Sunday school teacher, he does not necessarily do his best. As a result of time and concerted effort, he improves. Also, teacher training programs for lay people in local churches have helped teachers improve their efforts.

Second, educational technique is not necessarily incompatible with the ministry of the Holy Spirit. If anything, the two go together, because God's plan in teaching is to use Christians — capable Christians — as instruments of the Holy Spirit. If God calls a man to preach, that calling does not exclude the necessity for his studying the science and art of sermon preparation and delivery. Christian teachers should learn all they can about how to be more effective in their important task. This may include the study of teaching techniques, educational theory, pupils' characteristics and development, the process of learning, lesson preparation and evaluation, the use of teaching aids, and so on. It may involve visiting others' classes, observing how others teach, reading about teaching, attending teachers' meetings and conferences. It should include gaining new insights into the truths of God's Word, the way God has made pupils act and think, how God causes pupils to learn, and how to communicate the truth of God effectively. The Holy Spirit works best through the teacher who knows these factors in the teaching-learning process and who works in cooperation with God in the process.

Third, to develop one's teaching gift can in no way improve the quality or essence of what God has given. Development is simply for the purpose of enlarging the effectiveness of the gift. It is not a matter of adding inherent quality to the gift, but rather expanding its usefulness. It is not a matter of adding good to that which is bad or only partially good, but rather adding growth to that which is implanted, development to that which is undeveloped, fruition to that which is latent. The parable of the talents in Matthew 25: 14-30 illustrates the importance, in God's sight, of effectively using what God has entrusted, rather than letting it lie dormant and passive. The man who buried his one "talent" was not rewarded, whereas those with five or ten "talents" saw their entrustment multiply and were rewarded by their master. Seeking to develop one's gift of teaching and thus multiply his efforts is pleasing to God. If a Christian is not interested in developing his gift, he is not a good steward. The teacher who feels he no longer needs to improve endangers the effectiveness of his ministry.

Another fact concerning the exercising of the gift of teaching should be highlighted. The Bible does not suggest that there are different gifts for specific age-groups, such as the gift of working with children or the gift of young people's work.[14] The teaching gift is a God-given ability, not the age-group where that ability may be used. However, it may safely be stated that the teaching gift, in some or perhaps most cases, may best be exercised with a certain age-group, because of the teacher's background, interests, and aptitudes. A Christian who has the gift of teaching may find that because of his interests, background, or personality, he can exercise that gift to one age-group better than to another.

Is the spiritual gift of teaching always necessary? Do not some inherently have a natural inclination or "knack" for teaching? Christians who apparently have this natural inclination for teaching either have the spiritual gift and may not realize it, or are exercising a spiritual gift in accord with a natural ability in teaching. Or this "knack" may be the result of exercising the gift over a period of time, so that now the gift is used with more ease and skill.

Several implications stem from this truth about the gift of teaching.

First, not everyone can teach the Bible. Not all Christians in positions of teaching necessarily possess the gift of teaching. Therefore, Sunday school and church leaders should select their teachers with care.

Second, every Christian should do his utmost to determine what his spiritual gift is, and then seek to be in a place of service where he can develop and exercise that gift, whatever it may be (1 Ti 4:14; 2 Ti 1:6).

Third, effective Sunday school teaching (and teaching in other Christian institutions) depends on teachers who have the spiritual gift of teaching. If the Holy Spirit has not given the gift of teaching to the one who is teaching, he will never be an effective teacher.

Fourth, local churches should do all they can to help believers determine and develop their spiritual gifts. This may mean counseling laymen and using them in various capacities of service.

Fifth, teacher training courses, in-service training, leadership training, and other training programs have definite, though indirect, biblical warrant.

Sixth, in-service assistant teaching or substitute teaching can be a means of helping Christians determine if they have the spiritual teaching gift, before they are given full positions of leadership responsibility.

Seventh, if teachers are ineffective, either they do not have the teaching gift, or are not developing it, or are not in fellowship with the Lord.

Eighth, the twofold goal of all spiritual gifts should always be borne in mind: the edifying of the body of Christ, and ascribing glory to the Lord (1 Pe 4:11*b*).

Ninth, teaching God's truth should always be done in the power of the Spirit, and in the atmosphere and attitude of love (1 Co 13; Eph 4:15-16*b*).

Tenth, church leaders need to give more emphasis in their teaching and preaching to this all-important doctrine of spiritual gifts.

6

Distinctive Ministries of the Divine and the Human

THE FACT that God dispenses to some believers the gift of teaching is unquestionable evidence that He has designed to use human instruments in the process of imparting His truth to others. But what is the distinctive function of the human teacher in the educational process? What is the distinctive ministry of the Holy Spirit? In teaching, what does God's Spirit do that man cannot do? What part does man have in teaching for which God holds him responsible? Since learning and growing in the Christian life is a divine process in the spiritual lives of believers, what place does the human teacher have? Conversely, since Christian teaching is an educational task involving teachers and pupils, in what sense can Christian education be called a supernatural process?

It is incorrect to emphasize the supernatural element in Christian teaching to the exclusion of the place of the human instrument. It is equally wrong to stress the importance of the place of the human teacher to the exclusion of the divine work of the Spirit. Yet, the two must not be thought of as so blended that the place and function of each is blurred. Let us consider four areas in which the divine and the human should function distinctively, yet cooperatively, in Christian education:

The Divine and the Human with Regard to the Gift of Teaching

The Holy Spirit dispenses the gift of teaching to those whom He sovereignly chooses; whereas the responsibility of the human teacher is to discover that gift, and then develop and exercise it to God's glory. The Spirit unfolds the gift; the human teacher should utilize it. The Spirit dispenses the gift; the human teacher should discover and develop it.

The Divine and the Human with Regard to the Principles of Teaching

It is entirely erroneous to suppose that teachers devise the laws or principles of pedagogy. God, not man, created the laws of teaching and learning. God made pupils to learn according to certain patterns of development and response to certain inner and outer factors. When educators state these principles of learning and development, they are simply pointing up what they have discovered, not what they have created.

Therefore, every Christian teacher should determine to learn the proper laws or principles of teaching and learning that God has made. As he does, he is functioning in cooperation with the Holy Spirit.

The Divine and the Human with Regard to the Channel in Teaching

The Holy Spirit seeks to teach through human channels or instruments. Human teachers should seek to be under the full employment of the Spirit, as clean and capable instruments. Effective Christian teaching takes place to the extent that teachers allow the Spirit to speak through them and use them because "the Christian teacher in the local church is the mouthpiece of the Holy Spirit."[1]

Teachers are not free to teach what they please, because

in the final sense, it is not they who teach, but the Holy Spirit. As instruments of the divine Teacher, they teach what the Spirit of God has revealed in His Word.

Also, the Spirit seeks to supply guidance, power, illumination, and insight to teachers, who have the responsibility of utilizing this enablement. Teachers should not be lifeless, passive automatons. Instead they should be active, dynamic, vital channels, fully usable by the Spirit. God works through human instruments, yet without loss of individual personality on the part of the teachers. Nor does this imply that lesson preparation by teachers is no longer necessary. If anything, it increases the need for preparation, so that they may be fully capable of being led by the Spirit to meet problems, questions, needs, and comments that arise in the teaching situation.

Paul said, "It is God who worketh in you" (Phil 2:13). And "I labor also, striving according to His working, which worketh in me mightily" (Col 1:29). "It is our talent that the Spirit uses, our insights, our enthusiasm, our hands — but it is His use of them that makes all the difference between wasted blight and jumbo harvest."[2] What a privilege to be instruments of, and yet colaborers with, God the Holy Spirit! Christian teachers ought to thrill at the thought of having a part in God's work.

Such a privilege behooves Christian teachers to be filled by the Spirit of God. This adds divine dynamic and spiritual power to the ministry of Christian teaching. Without the spiritual impact of a yielded life, the Christian teacher's efforts are relatively futile. With it, his efforts become marvelously fruitful.

THE DIVINE AND THE HUMAN WITH REGARD TO THE WORD OF GOD

The Holy Spirit transforms the outer Word into inner experiences,[3] whereas the task of human teachers is to *pro-*

claim to others the outer Word and to *portray* it in their own inner experience. Only the Holy Spirit of God is capable of reaching and molding the pupils' inner beings. Only He can take the outer Word and make it relevant and operative in the hearts and souls of pupils. LeBar expresses this beautifully:

> No other teacher can be both an outer and an inner factor. No other teacher can get inside the pupil to perform a personal, intimate operation in the depths of his being. As God's active agent or method, the Spirit does subjectively within the pupil all that Christ has done objectively without. Educational method is simply finding out how the Spirit works and working with Him rather than against Him, as we so often do even with the best of intentions. As the human teacher works with the divine Teacher, the Scriptural record becomes more than letters and sounds and words; it becomes the living voice of God speaking to the heart.[4]

Only the Holy Spirit can do this. But the place of Christian teachers is by no means ruled out. Teachers can influence inner factors only by manipulating the outer. It is the responsibility of every teacher to work with the Spirit and thus be used by Him to effect inner changes. Both the teachers' lessons and living should be such that the Holy Spirit can use them to apply truth and stimulate spiritual growth.

This raises the question, Who applies the truth to learners? Do teachers? Do learners? Does the Holy Spirit? Actually, it may be said that all three "apply" the truth, but each in a different sense. Teachers have the responsibility of pointing out, or expounding, truths to be applied, as well as areas in pupils' lives where truth should be applied. Learners, on the other hand, apply the truth in the sense that they see the need for the truth to be related to their lives, yield to the work of the Spirit, and receive the Spirit's ministry to them. The Holy Spirit, however, is the only one who can apply truth in the sense of personalizing the truth to individuals, or injecting the truth into the reality of pupils' experiences. Teachers present the Word, pupils receive and appropriate it, the Spirit relates it to pupils and transforms lives by it.

This is not to say, however, that teachers need to be concerned only about declaring the truth, without any concern for heart-needs of pupils. Teaching includes both the declaring of truth and the guiding of pupils. It is erroneous for teachers to suppose that all they need to do is unfold Scripture and let the Holy Spirit apply it where it is needed. There is a dangerous half-truth in such a statement. True, the Holy Spirit does apply to the experience the truth that has been taught. But He does so only with truth that has been chosen discriminately with relation to life-needs and in cases where the heart soil has been prepared to receive the seed of the Word of God. Scriptural truths scattered indiscriminately will inevitably fall on stony ground, thorny ground, or "by the wayside." Bible truths chosen and presented by teachers on the basis of life-needs and on prepared "soul soil" can be used to the fullest by the Spirit.

The intricate interweaving of the human and divine elements is evident in 1 Corinthians 2:1—4:7. For instance, man should preach and teach not with brilliance of speech or intellect, but in the demonstration of the Spirit's power. The human part involves setting forth spiritual truths in words, but the Spirit unveils things never seen, shares the deepest truths of God, and gives insight into God's grace. Man waters, but God gives the growth. The Christian teacher is a temple and a steward, but the Spirit indwells.

This teaching process, dualistically involving the divine and the human, implies that Christian teachers should fulfill these responsibilities:

First, learn how God works in teaching (know teaching principles) and then work with God.

Second, depend on the Spirit to guide them and empower

their teaching. Education should always occur in dependence on God.

Third, utilize and develop their spiritual gifts.

Fourth, be concerned for their pupils' growth and development.

Fifth, motivate their pupils and help them learn.

Sixth, live exemplary Christian lives and be usable by the Spirit in guiding their pupils.

In this educational partnership in which the human teacher and the Holy Spirit each have distinctive functions, it must be remembered that in the final analysis, God is the Teacher. The human teacher in his finiteness is limited. Christian educators must recognize that the ultimate objectives of Christian education cannot be achieved in their own power. Christian teaching is a divine work in which the Teacher and Guide is God Himself. He supplies the truth. He aids teachers in teaching the truth, and learners in learning it. Thus, "Christian education is more than a human enterprise."[5] Every Christian teacher must grant that it is ultimately "God that giveth the increase" (1 Co 3:7). Teaching, like any aspect of Christian service, is "not by might, nor by power, but by my Spirit, saith Jehovah of hosts." (Zec 4:6).

7

The Spiritual Life of the Human Teacher

IF THE HOLY SPIRIT is operative in Christian teaching, then why do teachers often fail to teach and pupils often fail to learn? The answer is that God has chosen to work through imperfect human instruments. Of the four basic factors in Christian teaching — the Holy Spirit, the Word of God, the teacher, and the pupil — the first two are perfect and infallible, and the other two are fallible and imperfect. The first two are invariable, and the other two variable. Therefore, if learning does not occur, it is the fault of either the teacher or the pupil, or both — not the fault of God's Spirit or God's Word. To the extent that the teacher or learner fails, the teaching process fails.

Human teachers are in a key position, capable of either facilitating or hindering learning. *What* and *how* they teach are vitally important. And their lives are important too — as important as the truth they teach orally. As Benson has reminded Christian leaders, "the example of a consistent Christian life counts more toward helping others reach a higher standard than any amount of instruction."[1]

And Cairns writes:

> The example of a radiant, honest, scholarly personality must accompany this basic practical as well as theoretical

86

intellectual theistic orientation. Students usually remember the teacher long after the data of the subject have been forgotten.[2]

This is not to belittle for a moment the absolute necessity of God's Word. Without it, Christian education is impossible. But it is to say that the truths of God's Word should be taught and communicated through lives that exemplify the Word and exalt Christ.

Teachers whose lives are not yielded to the Holy Spirit and in whom there is unconfessed sin prevent the effective teaching ministry of the Spirit through them. Sin will hamper both the power of their influence *with* their students and the effectiveness of their presentation of truth *to* their students. Many teachers have admitted that at times their teaching has not been well received simply because of sin in their own lives. Even though all other factors in the teaching situation may be conducive to learning, sin in teachers' lives decreases the possibility of learning. Even though Christian teachers possess the gift of teaching, the extent of their effectiveness depends on their being controlled by the Holy Spirit.

Every teacher should so live and teach that he can testify as did the apostle Paul concerning his ministry among the Thessalonians: "Our gospel came not unto you in word only, but also in power, and in the Holy Spirit, and in much assurance; even as ye know what manner of men we showed ourselves toward you for your sake" (1 Th 1:5). This verse outlines the pattern that every teacher should follow in his teaching ministry. The teacher's *content* ("our gospel," "the Word"), the teacher's *communication* ("in power," "in the Holy Spirit," "in much assurance") and the teacher's *conduct* ("what manner of men we were among you") are all important. What a teacher teaches, how he teaches, and how he lives should harmonize to make his ministry scriptural and dynamic.

The exemplary spiritual lives of teachers involve, on their

part, a personal experiencing of the truth. If they are teaching a scriptural portion, they should have experienced, or should be experiencing, this truth themselves. If they are teaching a so-called secular subject, they ought to have experienced, or be experiencing, the implications of the Christian viewpoint on that subject.

It is important that Bible truths being taught be a part of teachers' lives so that they will know whereof they speak, will be concerned about the truth they are teaching, and will make an impact on the lives of their pupils. Those lessons that make an impact on pupils' lives are those that have first made an impact on the lives of teachers. If Christian teachers delve in truth without relating it to their spiritual experience, their pupils may see little need for living the truth. Many teachers in this way limit the Spirit's working through them.

Christian teachers must be in vital union with Christ. They must love Him and His Word. Their personal acquaintance with and deep love for Christ are essential. This must be ranked above their knowledge of things, books, or men.

These words addressed by Paul to Timothy should be pondered by every Christian teacher: "Take heed to thyself, and to thy teaching" (1 Ti 4:16). It is not enough for teachers to be concerned only with their lives or only with the doctrines they teach. They must be concerned with both. This responsibility is basic to harmonious cooperation between the human and the divine in the glorious ministry of Christian teaching.

Part 3

THE HOLY SPIRIT
AND THE BIBLE

What place should the Bible have in Christian education? What should be the final authority in Christian teaching? What should be the center of the curriculum? Should evangelical teaching be transmissive or progressive? If teachers are teaching in cooperation with the Spirit, does this mean that their interpretations of the Bible are accurate?

8

The Bible as the Authority

WHAT CRITERION or standard should teachers follow in determining the material to teach and the activities in which to engage their pupils? What authoritative guide should pupils accept in testing the conflicting voices that seek to tell them what to believe and do? What should be the final voice of authority in Christian education? Should it be the church? Teachers? Pupils' experiences? The Holy Spirit? The Bible?

Because "the problem of authority is the most fundamental problem that the Christian church ever faces,"[1] Christian teachers need to consider this problem carefully. Several views about authority in evangelical teaching are current.

THE CHURCH AS AUTHORITY

Some people claim that the final authority for faith and life is the official teaching of the institutional church. This view is held by Roman Catholicism and a few Protestant groups.

The Roman Catholic church accepts the Bible as authoritative, but insists that it alone is not a safe guide. Oral tradition supplies what is lacking in written tradition, the Scriptures, and thus is an authority alongside the Bible. Tradition is authoritative because it testifies to the inspiration and preservation of Scripture, and because it was appealed to by the church fathers in order to refute heresies and settle controversies.[2] To Roman Catholics, the church is the final authority because it is the custodian, guardian, teacher, and interpreter of the Bible, and the custodian and preserver of oral tradition. The church is the interpretive authority in all matters of faith and morals, and its pronouncements must be accepted without question.

The following arguments fully decimate the possibility of church tradition, whether written or oral, having final authority:

First, ecclesiastical tradition often contradicts itself, thus destroying its claimed authority.

Second, church tradition often contradicts Scripture. This then necessitates a choice of one or the other as final and authoritative. Since church tradition is often self-contradictory, it is conclusive that Scripture stands as sole authority over tradition.

Third, tradition removes the boundaries of revelation and makes the authority of God equivocal. Tradition is nebulous, unlimited, and therefore without a clear ring of authority.

Fourth, tradition places the church above the Bible. But the church as a corporate body or council did not give the Bible to the world. God gave the Bible, but He used individuals, not a hierarchy or an institution, to pen His inspired Word.

> Calvin insisted that the Church is governed by the Word and the Spirit, and therefore must be in subjection to the Scriptures. All traditions and the entire ecclesiastical hierarchy must submit to this lordship.[3]

Fifth, church tradition cannot be the final authority for Christian education because it has numerous differing viewpoints, all of which point to a human, subjective authority. When authority is subjective, based on man's opinions, it is inadequate. Calvin highlights this fact by saying that "our faith would have too weak a foundation if we had only the authority of men."[4] He opposes ecclesiastical authority because it makes the truth of God dependent on "the arbitrary will of men."[5] The voice of the church concerning Scripture is still the voice of man.

Teachers as Authority

Another approach to the problem of authority is the view that teachers and scholars are to be respected as having the voice of final authority in matters pertaining to Christian living and Christian education. They are the final determinants and guides in structuring an educational curriculum. Packer describes this position:

> Hence, just as the Medievals tended to equate Church tradition with the Word of God, so modern Protestants tend to equate the words of scholars with the Word of God. We have fallen into the habit of accepting their pronouncements at second hand without invoking the Spirit's help to search Scripture and see, not merely whether what they say is so (in so far as the lay Bible student is qualified to judge this), but also — often more important — whether God's Word does not deal with more than the limited topics with which scholars at any one time are concerned. The result of this negligence is widespread ignorance among Churchmen as to what Scripture actually says.[6]

Teachers of this kind tend to promote static learning and to suppress pupil expression in the learning of truth. This was one of the chief complaints voiced by Dewey against traditional secular education. This complaint applied equally well to Christian education. According to Dewey,

> The traditional scheme is, in essence, one of imposition from above and from outside. It imposes adult standards, subject matter, and methods upon those who are . . . growing . . . toward maturity.

He continued by stating that

> the very situation forbids much active participation by pupils in the development of what is taught. Theirs is to do — and learn, as it was the part of the six hundred to do and die. Learning here means acquisition of what already is incorporated in books and in the heads of the elders. Moreover, that which is taught is thought of as essentially static.[8]

Though Christian educators do not accept many of Dewey's concepts, they do recognize that his complaint merits some thoughtful consideration.

For teachers to prescribe what pupils shall uncritically accept, is to border on authoritarianism, which, it must be clarified, is different from authority. Christians have an *authoritative* message which should not be confused with *authoritarian* method. LeBar clarifies this distinction:

> The major problem in relation to authoritative revelation is to get it accepted by each new generation. *Authoritarian* method is often associated with our *authoritative* message. If the Bible is taught in the spirit of "Here it is; you take it because I say so"; if it is taught by stereotyped, rote-memory methods, what happens? Instead of accepting it as their own conviction, young people rebel against this affront to their free will. Likewise we fail if we try to transmit Scripture by transmissive methods, if we only ask young people to parrot it back to us in the form in which we gave it.[9]

Evangelical Christian educators do not accept the position that teachers or scholars are the authority in education, because this borders on authoritarianism, stifles pupil creativity and learning, and makes the acceptance of truth superficial.

EDUCATIONAL EXPERIENCE AS AUTHORITY
(PROGRESSIVE EDUCATION)

According to John Dewey, the authoritative norm in education is the experience of the pupils. He did not discard authority altogether; he simply shifted the source of authority from the external teacher to the internal experiences of pupils. Dewey advocated expression and cultivation of individuality rather than imposition from above. He advocated learning through experience rather than from texts and teachers. Dewey stressed that the aim of education is the continuous reconstruction of experience, and that the center of the curriculum is the pupil's own social activities. Of course experience is a part of the educative curriculum, but it is erroneous from the evangelical viewpoint to hold that "education is a development within, by, and for experience"[10] and nothing more.

This view of experience in education stems from Dewey's underlying empirical naturalism in which he repudiated the belief in an authoritative moral or spiritual truth.

Dewey's emphasis on experience, along with later developments in the field of psychology, influenced religious educators to see the importance of understanding the response of the people being taught as well as the subject matter they were seeking to teach. This resulted, in many circles, in a shift of the seat of authority from subject matter to pupil experiences. "So religious education began to turn to curricula designed with the needs and abilities and experiences of its pupils as a guiding principle."[11] Thus some religious educators have gone so far as to say that "the source of authority is in the educational process itself."[12]

To accept the experience of pupils as the core of authority in education is to accept a subjective and therefore nonreliable norm. It places education in the quagmire of experimentalism, and leaves man without any infallible source of truth.

Christian education involves far more than experience; it begins with the supernatural message of God's truths, His infallible written revelation, the Bible. The Bible is God's objective revelation of Himself and His purposes to man. It is His communication to man by which He seeks to transform human experience into Christlike living, on the basis of salvation through faith in Christ. The Bible is the judge of educational experience, not vice versa. Therefore, in the curriculum of Christian education, experience alone cannot be consulted as the final court of appeal.

RELIGIOUS EXPERIENCE AS AUTHORITY
(LIBERALISM AND NEOLIBERALISM)

According to liberalism, God contacts man through religious experience. In his subjective religious faculties, man knows God and thus has his authority within his own soul.

> The specific essence of religious experience may be feeling (Schleiermacher), valuation (Ritschl), filial piety or prayer (Sabatier), or ecstasy (mysticism), but in and through this subjective experience God gives Himself.[13]

In liberalism, man's reason or rationalistic experience serves as a check on revelation. Sabatier expresses the sentiments of religious liberals regarding the authoritative nature of religious experience and reason:

> Moses, Isaiah, Paul, John, Peter, are to me and will continue to be, in the religious order, men of God clothed with a very great moral authority; I put myself to school with them, I profit by their lessons, they are incomparable models and previous teachers; but, after all, I am still free to choose between their ideas, to criticize their reasonings, to reject such of their teachings as are to me unassimilable.[14]

Burrows accepts the principle that "what is ultimately authoritative for us is that which commands the assent of our own best judgment, accepted as the witness of the Spirit within us."[15]

This view leaves man without any evaluative norm of judgment. He stands without any intelligent basis for his so-called faith. Each man accepts as authority that which is right in his own eyes. This actually puts an end to any kind of final, objective authority.

EXISTENTIAL ENCOUNTER AS AUTHORITY (NEOORTHODOXY)

Neoorthodoxy implies that man's subjective response to God's revelation is the ultimate determinant of spiritual truth. Neoorthodoxy maintains that authority is not in the Bible and that the Bible is not the Word of God, unless it is met by the existential response of man in a divine-human encounter. The Bible is simply a fallible record of revelation and becomes the Word of God only when it speaks to the human soul. God does not give propositions of truth about Himself; He reveals Himself. The Bible is not revelation; it becomes revelation only when man responds to God's encounter in which He, not information about Him, is revealed.

Because man's active response to the record of revelation supposedly guarantees the Bible's validity, man becomes his own standard for determining what in the Bible is the Word of God. He stands in judgment on the Bible; and therefore his experience, not the Bible, is his authority or guiding principle.

According to neoorthodoxy, the Bible is both "witness" and "instrument." As witness, it is the record of God's past revelatory events, and as instrument it is the revelatory means whereby God today speaks His Word.[16] Barth explains the work of the Holy Spirit in reference to revelation as a work of preparation for receiving the revelation as God's Word. The Holy Ghost as the "finger of God" is "the subjective aspect in the conception of revelation"[17] by which His Word becomes truth to man.

The neoorthodox position of revelation and authority cannot be accepted by Evangelicals for the following reasons:

First, neoorthodoxy leaves man without a normative

criterion of truth, and sets him adrift on the sea of speculations and doubts. Man is asked to accept the trustworthiness of a spiritual experience which is based on an untrustworthy Bible record. As Finlayson argues:

> We are left in the impossible position of having to accept as true as a matter of religious experience what we must reject as false as a matter of objective reality. In no other department of human thought or research is truth based on subjective experience that lacks objective reality, yet this is what is offered us as the basis of religion.[18]

Second, the idea of revelation as encounter borders on mysticism and immediacy of the Spirit. The Bible serves only as the frame within which the Spirit existentially encounters man. The experience of an ineffable encounter most obviously leads to mysticism.

Third, divine authority cannot reside in a human, fallible Bible. If the Bible is a human, errant document, it is questionable how it can serve, with any degree of reliability, as a witness or instrument to point men to a personal knowledge of God. At best all the neoorthodox Christian educator can do is seek to place his pupils in positions (whatever they may be!) where they can respond to God's encounter.

Fourth, neoorthodoxy does not even give man a standard for guaranteeing that he has apprehended the reality of revelation itself.

The Bible as Authority (Evangelicalism)

No curriculum of evangelical Christian education can be set up, with any degree of certainty, permanency, or adequacy, on the basis of ecclesiastical or educational authoritarianism, or the educational, religious, or existential experiences of teachers or pupils. Something more reliable, more objective, and more normative must be accepted as authority.

This norm, Evangelicals believe, is the Bible, God's written revelation.

Orthodoxy has consistently maintained that authority ultimately rests with God. As Creator and Sustainer of the universe, He has the absolute right over all created beings and all-embracing authority in heaven and earth. As the second Person of the Trinity, Jesus Christ possesses divine authority. "All authority hath been given unto me in heaven and on earth" (Mt 28:18). "He taught them as having authority" (Mk 1:22). This imperial, veracious authority of God is expressed to man not through the church, nor religious experiences, but through divine self-revelation. Because of man's finiteness, God as ultimate authority cannot be apprehended directly by man. So God's authority had to be mediated through a delegated authority. Because God has revealed Himself through the Scriptures, the Bible is divinely authoritative, possessing divinely *delegated* authority. This is cause and effect: the Bible is God's revelation to man, and therefore it is authoritative.

The Bible is the special revelation of God in written "God-breathed" form. Both the Old and New Testaments were considered as the written revelation of God. In John 10:35 the Word of God and Scripture are identified as one. In Romans 16:25-26, revelation is identified with "the Scriptures of the prophets." Paul's epistles are recognized by Peter as coauthoritative with "the other Scriptures" (2 Pe 3:15-16). In one verse Paul quotes from both the Old Testament and New Testament and refers to the passages as "the Scripture" (1 Ti 5:18).

Christ recognized the authority of the Old Testament as God's written revelation. "Till heaven and earth pass away, one jot or one tittle shall in no wise pass away from the law" (Mt 5:18). "The scripture cannot be broken" (Jn 10:35). "Think not that I came to destroy the law or the prophets" (Mt 5:17). His life ministry, crucifixion, and resurrection were in fulfillment of the authoritative Old Testament.

The apostles also recognized the authority of Scriptural revelation. "Whatsoever things were written aforetime were written for our learning" (Ro 15:4; cf. 1 Co 10:11). They quoted the Old Testament as the Word of God (Ac 4:25; Ro 9:17); they recognized the authority of Christ's teachings (Ac 20:35; 1 Co 7:10); they claimed an authoritative commission from Christ (Gal 1:1); they were joined in rank with the Old Testament prophets (2 Pe 3:2); and their God-inspired writings came from the authoritative voice of God (1 Co 14:37; Gal 1:8; 1 Th 2:13; 2 Th 2:15, 3:14; 1 Jn 1:1-5).

Christians accept the Bible as their authoritative guide and rule for faith and conduct because it is an objective revelation, an infallible norm, and the efficacious truth of God (Jn 17:17; 1 Th 2:13). The Bible furnishes man with an absolute standard and test of truth. As such, it contains propositions of truth about God, and through the Holy Spirit, brings man into loving relationship with the person of God. Whether man receives the Bible as his authority does not affect the authoritative quality of the Bible. It stands as the infallible authority of truth, regardless of man's attitude toward it.

Archbishop Temple rejects the concept of propositional revelation on several counts, one of which is that if Christians are to regard the Bible as a body of infallible doctrines, they need an infallible human interpreter to tell them what it means.[19] However, this is a non sequitur argument. Why should the Bible need an infallible interpreter when it is already infallible? The infallibility of the Word of God is not vitiated by fallible interpreters who seek merely to comprehend its truths without ascribing authority to it. Furthermore, believers do have, in a sense, an infallible interpreter — the Holy Spirit. The Holy Spirit, the true church's infallible Teacher, guides believers into the meaning of Scripture, aids them in determining laws for interpreting it, and "we measure all human pronouncements on Scripture by Scripture's own statements."[20]

Some teach that the Christian's authority is not Scripture, but Christ, who is above it as its Judge. They say that Christians must judge Scripture by Him and accept only what is in harmony with His life and teaching. Framer calls "the living Christ speaking through the Holy Spirit"[21] the final and absolute authority for the faith and life of the church. Grimes states that "the pivot of authority is the event of Jesus Christ — God entering into and acting through history to speak a living word to man's questions and needs."[22] This view is unsatisfactory for the following reasons:

First, it leaves man without an objective means of ascertaining the voice of Christ's authority. Christ's authority is made explicit to the church today only through God's written revelation. The Bible is the only adequate source by which men may gain an understanding of God. "If it be alleged that Christ is the one Authority, yet it is through a critical study of the Scriptures, apart from subjective prejudice, that the knowledge of Christ is to be obtained."[23]

Second, Christ used His personal authority to endorse and confirm the authority of the Old Testament. Christ is the ultimate Authority, but it is through the Bible that He now exercises His divine authority, imparting authoritative truth. The Bible is clothed with His authority. Therefore, in a sense, both Christ and the Bible are authority. Packer argues cogently to this point:

> Certainly, He is the final authority for Christians: that is precisely why Christians are bound to acknowledge the authority of Scripture. Christ teaches them to do so. A Christ who permits His followers to set Him up as the Judge of Scripture, One by whom its authority must be confirmed before it becomes binding and by whose adverse sentence it is in places annulled, is a Christ of human imagination, made in the theologian's own image, one whose attitude to Scripture is the opposite to that of the Christ of history.[24]

Another question is sometimes raised in reference to the Bible's authority: Do not the Holy Spirit and the Bible together comprise a dual authority? Ramm's answer is in the affirmative: "The Holy Spirit speaking in the Scripture . . . is the principle of authority for the Christian Church."[25] But this view leads to the idea that if the Holy Spirit does not speak in the Bible, the Bible is not authoritative. As previously noted, the Bible *alone* is fully authoritative, because it is God's inspired revelation. This is the reformers' position on *sola scriptura*.

With Ramm it is agreed that the *pattern* of authority consists of Christ, the Word, and the Holy Spirit,[26] but this must not convey the notion that the Word does not bear authority apart from the Holy Spirit. When the Spirit is conjoined with the Word, He does not *give* it authority; He appropriates the truth to the human heart, and thus makes the Word of God efficaciously *operative*. The authority of the Word is then recognized by the believer. The Spirit witnesses to this authority, but He does not ascribe authority to the Bible. As Thomas explains, "The Spirit does not *constitute* the authority but rather *testifies* to its authority."[27]

The divine authority of the written Word is the "distinctive mark of true Christianity,"[28] and the only basis for an adequate curriculum in true Christian education. Education that bypasses the central finality of God's Word is not evangelical Christian education.

Without scriptural revelation as the final authority in Christian education, each pupil is left on his own to carve his own path through the labyrinth of ideas in the search for truth.

The Bible is more than a resource among resources "to be used in validating and evaluating the sources of encounter with God."[29] Instead, it is the only authoritative norm in Christian education. The Bible is the foundation and basis of Christian teaching.

Because Christian educators accept God's scriptural revelation as final, ultimate authority, it follows that God's written Word should be accepted as the primary source of the guiding principles for Christian education.

Christian educators are amiss when they borrow principles of education from sources such as reason, experience, or man-made educational systems. God's distinctive revelation — the Bible — is the distinctive source from which educational principles should be drawn. LeBar laments that failure to do this has resulted in lack of spiritual reality in Christian teaching:

> A chief reason for the lack of life and power and reality in our evangelical teaching is that we have been content to borrow man-made systems of education instead of discovering God's system. Secular educators do not give central place to the unique revelation of God's Word that is communicated by God's Spirit. Our distinctive content calls for distinctive treatment.[30]

The reason evangelical educators cannot accept secular education as its source of principles is that it is often at variance with Scripture, the believers' ultimate authority. Secular educational principles are often built on unscriptural philosophical bases such as pragmatism, empiricism, and naturalism. When there is conflict or variance in principles, Christian educators need to go back to their divine source to be sure that the principles they have formulated are drawn from or consistent with Scripture.

The Bible is not a textbook on education, but it does include insights into educational philosophy and method. Because God made the learner, his teacher, his content, and his environment, Christians look to God and His Word, rather than to erring secularists for valid educational concepts.

9

The Bible as the Basic Content

BECAUSE THE BIBLE is the authority for Christian education, it is the source of educational principles. But it is also the essential content of Christian education. Too often, religious education has greatly neglected the place of content, as Bower, a liberal religious educator, admits.[1] The content of the written Word of God is important because it makes plain God's will for man. Christian education concerns itself with Bible content because through it persons are brought into direct, personal contact with the living God.

For this reason, Christian education is *transmissive*. Christian teachers have a Book to teach, God's divine Word to communicate, a written revelation to make known. God's truths are not hidden in the inner recesses of man's nature, to be drawn out by experienced teachers. Nor are they there in seminal form, waiting to be developed under the influence of proper environment. God's truth is to be perpetuated by transmissive teaching, as clearly indicated in verses such as Exodus 10:2; Deuteronomy 6:6-9, 20; 31:11-13; Psalm 78:2-7; Luke 24:27, 32; Acts 8:4, 28:31; and 2 Timothy 2:2, 3:15.

Unregenerate men are totally ignorant of God's truths. Their religious concepts are garbled by sin, and they are blind to the truth of God (Ro 1:19-32; 1 Co 2:6-14). Therefore, this truth must be transmitted to them if they are to know Christ, who is the way, the truth, and the life.

The Bible is "propositional," containing statements or propositions of truth about God and His dealings with man. Those propositions are not written systematically in textbook form, but are related to experiences recorded in the Bible. It is impossible for God to reveal Himself to man without revealing at the same time something of His character, attributes, or purposes. Biblical revelation is both propositional *and* personal, rather than simply one or the other. Propositional truths about God are revealed in the Bible, as indicated in 2 Samuel 7:27, Isaiah 22:14, Amos 3:7, and Matthew 11:25 and 16:17. Personal knowledge of God is stressed in Philippians 3:10. But both truth about God, and God Himself as a person are revealed in 1 Samuel 3:11, 21.

Transmissive Bible teaching is decried by many schools of thought as unsound and unrealistic. It is claimed that the transmission of Bible truth makes teaching noncreative, limits the content to a prescribed "given" body of content, and is irrelevant to pupils' experiences. But divine authority demands human creativity. There is no reason why Bible teaching cannot be an exciting creative venture. When man has discovered God's truth, what would be the value of continuing the search? The "given" truth in Christian education liberates man into true Christian freedom (Jn 8:44). Furthermore, Christian truth is life-transforming. It is "profitable for teaching, for reproof, for correction, for instruction which is in righteousness: that the man of God may be complete, furnished completely unto every good work" (2 Ti 3:16-17).

The problem is that Christian teachers have not always indicated the Bible's relevance to life-needs and situations. Religious educators have spoken against transmissivism because to them it appears, as it did to Coe,[2] to lead to or be identical with dead orthodoxy.

Many Christian educators must plead guilty to this charge. Transmissivism *often does* lead to dead orthodoxy simply because the transmission of God's truth has been attempted apart from the power of the Holy Spirit. The mere intellectual mastery of Bible truths does not guarantee spiritual living. The truth must become a part of pupils' lives. But this can take place only by means of the inner working of the Holy Spirit. Transmissive teaching has a built-in power because of the presence and work of the Holy Spirit. Ineffective transmissive teaching does not imply that teachers should discard Bible content. Instead, it means they should seek to teach Bible content in the power and dynamic of God's Spirit.

This brings to light two extreme positions of thought regarding authoritative content and personal experience. Some religious educators emphasize mastery of subject matter, whereas others stress the development of pupils. The former is generally referred to as traditional transmissivism and the latter as progressivism. In the former, content is vital, and pupils have learned, it is presumed, when subject matter is memorized, understood mentally, and can be reproduced in written form for the teacher. The goal of Christian education, according to this view, is familiarity with Bible facts.

Other secular and religious liberal educators believe that the center of the curriculum ought to be the experiences of pupils. With an eye to the needs of pupils, these educators tend to exclude any fixed content from the curriculum.

Neither of these extreme positions gives proper place to the Holy Spirit. Poor traditional Christian education places such an overconfidence in the ability of transmitted subject matter to bring about learning that it tends to neglect the work of the Spirit in the teaching process. Progressivism, on the other hand, magnifies the place of pupil experience to the extent that the Spirit of God in the educative process is not deemed necessary.

Neither view is accurate. Neither content nor experience

can be omitted or minimized with impunity. In evangelical Christian education both content and experience are looked on as necessary — with Bible content as the basis of the curriculum.

Experience is the avenue of interaction in the learning process, which is guided by the Holy Spirit. In secular education, experience is totally human; in Christian education, experience, when it involves the interaction of pupils with the written Word and the living Word, takes on a *super-natural* nature.

But experience in education must have the right foundation. Experience not adequately based on the authoritative foundation of Scripture is empty mockery. With a wrong foundation, the possibility for right experience is canceled. This is one of the inadequacies of neoorthodoxy. The neo-orthodox theologian is interested in personal experience with God rather than simply a knowledge of facts about God. This is fine. But he seeks to gain this experience by means of existential encounter, apart from doctrinal truth. Thus he has no ground of objectivity and no assurance that his experience is valid.

According to the biblical view, man comes to know God experientially only by means of knowing Him conceptually. Experiential knowledge of God is possible only through conceptual knowledge of God (although conceptualism does not necessarily guarantee experientialism). Conceptualism becomes experientialism only when the pupil is receptive to the ministry of the Spirit. Valid Christian experience (whether it pertains to spiritual birth into the Christian life or to growth within the Christian life) cannot be obtained or maintained apart from valid Christian truth.

In evangelical Christian education, the curriculum is Christ-centered, Bible-based, and life-related.

The curriculum is *Christ-centered* in these senses:

First, Christ, the living Word (Jn 1:1), is central in the Bible, the written Word. *He* is the Saviour, the Lord, the

Friend, the Intercessor, the coming King on whom all Scripture is focused. Because Christianity is Christ, all Christian education should be centered and focused on Him.

Second, Christ is the goal of Christian living. Pupils are to "grow up in all things into him" (Eph 4:15), to know Him (Phil 3:10), to be conformed to His image (Ro 8:29), to be mature in Him (Col 1:28). Christlikeness is the goal toward which evangelical educators seek to lead their pupils.

Third, Christ is the source of strength for Christian teachers. They must look to Him for spiritual sustenance, gracious enablement, divine power. Only in Christ can they know the "exceeding greatness of [God's] power" (Eph 1:19).

The curriculum is *Bible-based* in the sense that the Scriptures constitute the basic content for Christian education. All curriculum materials and activities are to be faithful to and based squarely on the foundation of biblical truth. The Bible is the "given," the body of content to be transmitted. It is the "basis" of all evangelical Christian education.

The curriculum is *life-related* in the sense that Bible content is to be made relevant and become a part of pupils' experiences, by means of the teaching ministry of the Holy Spirit, in which He illuminates the minds and hearts of pupils and appropriates the Word to them. Bible teaching should be concerned with helping pupils know, feel, and do God's Word; to learn and live Bible truths; to know and love the Lord Jesus Christ personally and deeply.

Both Bible content and pupil experience are to be given proper consideration in Christian education materials and programs.

A number of scripture verses that emphasize the place of biblical content are:

> Wherewith shall a young man cleanse his way? By taking heed thereto according to thy *word* (Ps 119:9).
> Thy *word* have I laid up in my heart, That I might not sin against thee (Ps 119:11).

Thy *word* is a lamp unto my feet, And light unto my path (Ps 119:105).

And many were gathered together, so that there was no longer room for them, no, not even about the door: and he spake the *word* unto them (Mk 2:2).

Simon Peter answered him, Lord, to whom shall we go? thou hast the *words* of eternal life (Jn 6:68).

Believest thou not that I am in the Father, and the Father in me? the *words* that I say unto you I speak not from myself: but the Father abiding in me doeth his works (Jn 14:10).

If thou put the brethren in mind of these things, thou shalt be a good minister of Christ Jesus, nourished in the *words* of the faith, and of the good *doctrine* which thou has followed until now (1 Ti 4:6).

Holding to the faithful *word* which is according to the *teaching,* that he may be able both to exhort in the sound *doctrine,* and to convict the gainsayers (Titus 1:9).

The following verses emphasize the place of Christian experience (note the occurrence of the word *do* in many of these verses):

For Ezra had set his heart to seek the law of Jehovah, and to *do* it, and to teach in Israel statutes and ordinances (Ezra 7:10).

Whosoever therefore shall break one of these least commandments, and shall teach men so, shall be called least in the kingdom of heaven: but whosoever shall *do* and teach them, he shall be called great in the kingdom of heaven (Mt 5:19).

Teaching them to *observe* all things whatsoever I commanded you: and lo, I am with you always, even unto the end of the world (Mt 28:20).

If any man willeth to *do* his will, he shall know of the teaching, whether it is of God, or whether I speak from myself (Jn 7:17).

If ye know these things, blessed are ye if ye *do* them (Jn 13:17).

Ye are my friends, if ye *do* the things which I command you (Jn 15:14).

The things which ye both learned and received and heard and saw in me, these things *do*: and the God of peace shall be with you (Phil 4:9).

But be ye *doers* of the word, and no hearers only, deluding your own selves. For if any one is a hearer of the word and not a *doer,* he is like unto a man beholding his natural face in a mirror: for he beholdeth himself, and goeth away, and straightway forgetteth what manner of man he was. But he that looketh into the perfect law, the law of liberty, and so continueth, being not a hearer that forgetteth but a *doer* that worketh, this man shall be blessed in his *doing* (Ja 1:22-25).

To him therefore that knoweth to *do* good, and *doeth* it not, to him it is sin (Ja 4:17).

The Holy Spirit is related to the Bible in that Bible content is inspired by Him, should be taught under His guidance, and is to be communicated to pupils through teachers working in cooperation with Him.

Neoorthodox Christian educators advocate a "gospel-centered" curriculum. According to Wyckoff, the curriculum should center in "the gospel of God's redeeming activity in Jesus Christ,"[3] not in Christ, the Bible, the pupils, or the church. Little takes the same view. "Such a curriculum centers more on the message and purpose of the Bible than the exact text."[4] She says this because she believes that the Bible text contains errors. Flores agrees with this position when he suggests that Christian teachers should teach not the Bible, but the message of the Bible.[5] According to this concept, the content of Christian education is God's *acts* of revelation and the *meaning* of those acts.

This view is defective for three reasons:

First, it is guilty of reading into the word *gospel.* It decimates the clear biblical teaching that the good news is God's plan of salvation from sin by His grace, through faith in

Christ (1 Co 15:1-3). This neoorthodox view makes the gospel mean something else than the outworking of God's whole redemptive plan. To a neoorthodox person, the gospel is God's present acts, in which He reveals Himself directly to man in subjective existential encounter, through a fallible Bible.

Second, it makes man the authority over the Bible, rather than vice versa, since the reader of the Bible must determine what in the Bible points to God's "message" and what does not.

Third, it equivocates biblical content. According to neoorthodoxy, the Bible "message" is more important than the Bible "text" because the text contains errors. But if the text is unreliable, how can its message be reliable? If God cannot produce an infallible Book, errorless in its original writings, then how can one have confidence that the "message" of God's Book is any more reliable than the text?[6]

10

The Spirit and
Biblical Interpretation

THE ILLUMINATING MINISTRY of the Holy Spirit is an inner, spiritual process. But this raises a thorny question which has been of constant concern to the church: If true learning comes by the Spirit's inner working, does this mean that the understanding of Scripture is ultimately a subjective matter? If the Spirit interprets the Word privately to individual believers, how can one determine the correct view among several conflicting interpretations? If two men profess to be taught by the Spirit and yet hold different views on some basic scriptural issue, which view is valid?

It is granted with Moule that "the blessed Spirit is not only the true Author of the written Word but also its supreme and true Expositor."[1] But the question remains as to how the meaning of God's authoritative Word can be accurately discerned amid conflicting interpretations. If human interpretations confuse the clarity of the Word, is the Bible no longer authoritative? Is the law of consistency violated when one allows the right of private judgment and at the same time claims that his interpretations are right and another's wrong?

This is a vital issue because, as Parker explains, "there is no function assigned to the Spirit more important for us to understand than that by which He assures to the church a profound and correct interpretation of Scripture."[2] Eternal truth must be understood and correctly interpreted.

The element of fallibility exists in the art of interpretation, because fallen humanity is not unerring, and because Bible truths are not written in systematic form. Therefore, the allowance of the *right* of private judgment does not mean that all the *results* of private interpretation are accurate.

Let us consider four tests by which to judge human interpretations of the Word of God. However, these criteria should not be thought of as authorities above the Word. They are simply reliable tests by which to judge fallible interpretations of the infallible Book.

The first test is the spirituality of the interpreter. "He that is spiritual judgeth [discerneth] all things" (1 Co 2:15), but he that is carnal is not able to understand the Word (1 Co 3:1-3) and is "without experience of the word of righteousness; for he is a babe" (Heb 5:13). Accurate interpretation comes as a result of spiritual preparedness, through the Spirit.[3] The carnal believer is susceptible to making inaccurate interpretations of the Bible because his mind and heart are not in harmony with the Spirit. God reveals His truths by the Spirit only to spiritual Christians. As Chafer writes concerning believers, "carnality of life excludes them from understanding, or progressing in, the deep things of God."[4] The Spirit seeks to fill the learner so that he can properly understand and appropriate the Bible.

A second test is that of logical consistency. Two believers may both be spiritual, but one or both may be wrong in their understanding of a Bible passage because of failure to think through the passage logically. Two contradictory views may both be wrong, or one may be wrong, but they cannot both be correct. God cannot contradict Himself. Because He is God, the Holy Spirit does not teach conflicting views on any given Bible passage. The Spirit seeks to aid the Spirit-filled learner to think clearly and accurately. The interpreter "must employ principles of reasoning in making inductions, deductions, analogies, and comparisons."[5]

A third test by which to judge human interpretations of the Bible is the harmonization of Scripture with Scripture. "The basic notion of the analogy of faith is that there is one system of doctrine taught in the Holy Bible and only one."[6]

But it is conceivable that two Spirit-filled believers, thinking logically and comparing Scripture with Scripture, may still hold conflicting interpretations on some passages. Therefore, another test is needed.

This fourth test is the test of the stream of historic evangelical Christianity — a test frequently overlooked by Evangelicals. Packer believes that this test yields much valuable help in understanding what Scripture teaches:

> The Spirit has been active in the Church from the first, doing the work He was sent to do — guiding God's people into an understanding of revealed truth. The history of the Church's labor to understand the Bible forms a commentary on the Bible which we cannot despise or ignore without dishonoring the Holy Ghost.[7]

Ramm stresses the importance of this test of interpretation:

> If Christ has founded the Church and given it His Word; if the Holy Spirit is the Teacher of the faithful; if the Church is "the house of God . . . the pillar and ground of the truth" (1 Ti 3:15); *then every generation of Christian theologians must be prepared to take seriously the history of theology* (broadly interpreted to include symbols, councils, theologians, and treatises) *as possessing manifestations of the teaching ministry of the Holy Spirit.*[8]

This does not do violence to the right of private interpretation, because the history of theology does not dictate how one interprets the Bible; it simply suggests the general flow of biblical interpretation. The Spirit seeks to aid learners in ascertaining the historic stream of Christian thought. Therefore, Christians who ignore the history of theology and accept biblical interpretations that are clearly out of harmony with it, will be hampered in their ability to ascertain the truth of the Spirit in God's Word. Interpretive individualism leads to sectarianism.

All four tests are necessary. Each is a test of harmony: the interpreter's life must be in harmony with the Spirit; the interpreter's thinking must be in harmony with the laws of logical thinking; the interpreter's scriptural views must harmonize with the rest of Scripture; and his views must harmonize with the stream of Christian theology. If any one of these tests is disregarded, inaccurate views may be admitted, and the Bible content of Christian education may be susceptible to misinterpretation and insufficient application.

Part 4

THE HOLY SPIRIT IN THE
TEACHING-LEARNING PROCESS

THE HOLY SPIRIT'S TEACHING MINISTRY is needed in relation to the content and to the teacher. And it is also needed in relation to the process in which teachers teach and learners learn. Unless God's Spirit is operating in the teaching and learning activities, the educational process is not Christian. It is important to see how the Holy Spirit operates in, or is related to, these four aspects of the teaching-learning process: the goal of Christian teaching, the nature of learning, the laws of effective learning and teaching, and the use of methods and materials.

But this immediately raises a problem: Do principles of pedagogy conflict with the work of the Holy Spirit? If the Holy Spirit is ministering to pupils through dedicated teachers, why consider the laws or principles of teaching and learning? Benson gives one of the best answers to this problem:

> Is not the Holy Spirit dishonored by the teacher who seeks to be guided by the laws of pedagogy? Not at all. One does not dishonor the Holy Spirit in complying with the laws of gravitation. One does not dishonor the Holy Spirit in becoming acquainted with the laws which govern the working of the human mind. No one was more fully led by the Holy Spirit than our Lord Jesus Christ and yet no one more consistently observed the laws of pedagogy.[1]

11

What Is Teaching and Learning?

A CLEAR UNDERSTANDING of the goal or aim of Christian education is basic to effective teaching. In fact, the person who seeks success in any endeavor must have a clear and definite aim before him while he works. However, if God does the work, does the worker need to be concerned about aims?

The answer to this question is suggested by Eavey, who states that "teaching that lacks aim is poor teaching, even if it is characterized by the presence of many good qualities."[1]

Christian education has frequently been hampered not only by aimlessness or lack of clarity with reference to aims, but also by improper or inadequate aims. When asked, "What is the purpose of Christian teaching?" many teachers reply, "To teach the Bible." But this is inadequate as the *ultimate* goal.

Of course, Christian teaching involves the teaching of Bible facts. In a sense, it *is* true that the goal is "to teach the Bible" because the Bible is the essential body of content to be transmitted. But mental accumulation of doctrinal truths falls short of the ultimate goal of Christian education for three reasons:

First, knowledge is of little worth unless it can be applied and used in fruitful ways.

Second, knowing what is in the Bible does not guarantee

that the one who possesses that knowledge will love it, obey it, and apply it to his life. Many pupils can quote memory verses, but fail to live them out in their lives. The Pharisees of Jesus' day knew the Scriptures, and many unbelievers today have mastered Bible content but have been unchanged by its truths.

Third, Bible knowledge is but a means to an end, not an end in itself. Bible knowledge is a means of fostering spiritual growth, but it does not always guarantee it. Therefore, the goal of Christian teaching, while it certainly includes the impartation of Bible facts, must extend beyond that.

Most Christian educators concur that the one inclusive and ultimate aim of Christian teaching is "that the man of God may be complete, furnished completely unto every good work" (2 Ti 3:17). All Christian teaching should be directed to the one final aim of upbuilding those taught so that they develop in character. Teaching is not "giving out" information as much as it is guiding pupils into finding the truth for themselves.

Murch defines the aim as "fitting men to live in perfect harmony with the will of God."[2] Christian education is intended to bring pupils ever closer to "the measure of the stature of the fulness of Christ" (Eph 4:13). Paul expressed the goal of teaching this way: "Admonishing every man and teaching every man in all wisdom, that we may present every man perfect [mature] in Christ" (Col 1:28).

This spiritual maturity means *knowing* God personally (not simply knowing about Him) and *loving* Him (not simply learning of Him) with all one's heart, soul, mind, and strength (Mk 12:30). Spiritual maturity means being filled with the Holy Spirit and yielded to Christ (Ro 6:13). It means having one's life Christ-controlled. It means letting Christ be the center of one's life, influencing, penetrating, and directing every area. This includes one's personal life, homelife, school life, business life, social life. Thus Christianity is not one among many "compartments" of life; instead, it permeates all of life. The spiritually mature Christian is the one who says with Solomon, "In *all* thy ways acknowledge him" (Pr 3:6).

Several specific aspects of this ultimate goal of spiritual maturity include: helping your pupils increase in knowledge, improve in attitudes, grow in appreciations, develop in skills. Teaching is helping pupils gain new understandings, new insights, more information, changed attitudes, new points of view, new skills, deeper values. LeBar mentions several comprehensive objectives:

> Right relation to God the Father, Son, the Holy Spirit; knowledge and love and practical use of the Bible; formulation of a Christian world and life view; a progressively closer walk with Christ; assuming of responsibility in the church, for the lost everywhere, and in the civic community.[3]

Christian teaching is concerned with spiritual transformation. Teachers should be content with nothing less than spiritual change, with Christ-honoring results in every area of pupils' everyday experiences. Teachers should so teach that their pupils come to accept Christ as their Saviour, and walk with Him, grow in Him, know Him, serve Him, worship Him, and enjoy Him.

Here are three steps that lead to this ultimate goal, and which should permeate every aspect of the educational work of the church:

(1) *bring* pupils *to* Christ (evangelism)
(2) *build* them up *in* Christ (edification)
(3) *send* them out *for* Christ (service)

Obviously, one cannot accomplish these purposes apart from the empowering and guiding ministry of the Holy Spirit. Christian teachers, working toward the proper objectives in Christian education, recognize with Paul their insufficiencies and dependence on God: "Not that we are sufficient of ourselves, to account anything as from ourselves;

but our sufficiency is from God" (2 Co 3:5).* As Christ said, "Without me ye can do nothing" (Jn 15:5, KJV).

Because spiritual growth or Christian maturity is the goal of Christian education, all Christian teaching must be directed toward helping pupils learn and grow in the Christian life. In view of the fact that teaching is helping people learn, "the basic problem is not teaching, but learning."[4] Unless teachers discover how people learn, they will not be able to teach as they ought. The test of real teaching is real learning. Basically, a teacher has not taught if no one has learned.

Vieth stresses this matter of knowing the nature of learning:

> A worker in wood conforms to the laws of the material he is working with in order to produce the smoothness of surface, strength, shade of stain, and other qualities in his finished product. A worker with human beings is but using refined common sense when he complies with the laws of growth with which God has endowed his "material" in order to produce the highest quality of Christain character.[5]

In view of the goal of teaching previously discussed, learning is more than listening, reciting, or memorizing. Pupils have not necessarily learned if there is only a mental apprehension of truth without an actual experiencing of the truth, appropriated to their lives by the Holy Spirit. Facts not per-

---

*According to neoorthodoxy, the goal of teaching is encounter or confrontation of pupils directly with God, in which the Bible *becomes* (not *is*) the Word of God. A basic error in the neoorthodox view of the teaching-learning process is the concept that this process is revelational. "Of course, learning, in the broad sense, is revelational in that new truths, skills, or attitudes are made known or 'revealed.' But the teaching and learning of the Bible should be thought of as an illuminational process, not revelational. In other words, learning and appropriating the truths of God to one's life is not an act in which the Bible *becomes* revelatory; instead it is an act by which the Holy Spirit illuminates the heart in respect to that which *already* is a written revelation of and from God. Learning the facts of the Bible and having one's life changed by them is the Spirit's work of illumination, not revelation" (Roy B. Zuck, "The Educational Pattern of Neo-orthodox Christian Education," *Bibliotheca Sacra,* 119:348, October-December, 1962).

ceived, skills taught in isolation, and verbalisms presented to passive, unmotivated pupils fall short of effecting genuine spiritual growth. Learning is the process in which a pupil modifies his behavior, through the Spirit's enabling, to conform more to the will of God and the image of Christ.

This definition of learning is given by Vieth:

> True learning is an inward experience through which the pupil appropriates to his own life and character the new knowledge, insight, attitude, or skill in living which may be mediated to him by the educational process. He is like a tree which puts forth its leaves, blossoms, and fruit because of the inner life which is flowing through it, and not like a Christmas tree, to which others fix tinsel, shiny balls, and lights which are not really its own and never will be.[6]

According to LeBar, learning is an inner, active, continuous, and disciplined process.[7] It is inner in the sense that changes must take place in the pupils' inner lives through the meeting of their needs. It is active in the sense that learning takes place when pupils are participating, interacting, and discovering God's truths for themselves. Learning is continuous in the sense that it is a steady, growing, on-going process. It is disciplined in the sense that there is guidance, control, and authority in the teaching-learning situation.

Pupils learn best when teachers have established conditions favorable to the working of the Holy Spirit. As pupils recognize their needs, and submit to the teaching of the Holy Spirit in meeting those needs, learning takes place. The Holy Spirit is essential in the learning of God's truth, for pupils can learn nothing of spiritual significance unless they are taught of God. Pupils have not learned till the Holy Spirit has made the truths of God relevant to their life needs.

12

Principles of Learning
and the Work of the Spirit

WHAT FACILITATES LEARNING? What factors or conditions are necessary for effective learning? How do pupils best learn? How can teachers cooperate with the Holy Spirit's laws which govern good learning?

Pupils learn best when they are motivated, when the subject matter is relevant to them, when they are actively involved, and when they are ready to learn.

THE PRINCIPLE OF MOTIVATION

One key factor in the process of learning is motivation. This is perhaps the basic principle of learning. If there is no motivation, there is little or no learning. If one of two pupils, both equally capable of learning, learns and the other does not, it is evident that the one who learned wanted to learn or was motivated to learn, whereas the other was not.

Motivating learning simply means making learning desirable or desired. It is causing pupils to *want* to learn. It is important that Christian teachers understand this principle so that they can use proper motivational factors and can lead their pupils to want to learn, rather than coercing them to learn.

Motivation facilitates learning. When pupils are motivated to learn, they learn more quickly and the results are more lasting. The stronger the motivation, the more rapid and effective the learning.

Motivation is integrally related to interests and needs. Pupils' needs or innate drives, placed within pupils by the Lord Himself, prompt actions. Pupils learn best when they are interested and sense needs to be met. This suggests that teachers, with the aid of the Holy Spirit, seek to discover the needs of their pupils, relate those needs to the Word of God, and thus enjoy the results of seeing motivated pupils learn. Sometimes pupils sense their needs and are already motivated to learn. Other times teachers must make the pupils aware of their needs, before they will be motivated to learn. A sense of need is the starting point of all learning.

There are two kinds of motivation — extrinsic and intrinsic. Extrinsic motivation with its prizes or rewards is not the most desirable kind of motivation because it suggests that spiritual life is not worth seeking for its own sake. It implies that the Bible material to be studied is not important enough to study for its own worth. Extrinsic incentives often create only temporary motivation and do not always cause students to give their best to their study.

In contrast to extrinsic factors is intrinsic motivation which taps pupils' inner drives and urges and leads them to that which is worth knowing and doing for its own sake. This is the kind of motivation that the Holy Spirit seeks to generate in the lives of Christian pupils.

> The approval of the teacher, and more especially of the class, affords a better motive than prizes. The inner sense of satisfaction from duty well done is a better motive than approval of teacher and class. The inner joy of having pleased the Master is the highest of all motives and should be appealed to whenever possible.[1]

The chief intrinsic motive of the believer is, or should be, the motive to conform to the desires of the One who redeemed him.

How does the Holy Spirit relate to this matter of motivation? How does He motivate, if at all? There are several works that the Spirit of God performs with reference to pupil motivation:

First, He seeks to create in the pupils an awareness of their needs. He endeavors to help them sense their own personal weaknesses. This He can do for them only as they are open to His convincing and teaching ministries, through their study of the written Word, prayer, and self-evaluative meditation.

Second, He seeks to lead pupils to Christ and His Word for answers to their needs. He is waiting to supply all their needs according to God's riches in glory by Christ Jesus (Phil 4:19).

Third, the Holy Spirit seeks to use teachers in leading pupils to the highest motives. Teachers should cultivate an appreciation for the loftiest motives, so that pupils' deepest needs are met through the teaching of the Word.

Fourth, the Holy Spirit seeks to give spiritual orientation to the inner drives and urges of human nature. Humans desire and need new experiences, achievement, expression, approval, possession, and competition. Each of these has the potential for fulfillment in the spiritual realm. For example, pupils want approval. But, of course, they ought to be more motivated by approval from the Lord than by approval from parents, teachers, or friends. "We keep his commandments and do the things that are pleasing in *his* sight" (1 Jn 3: 22). "When a man's ways please Jehovah, He maketh even his enemies to be at peace with him" (Pr 16:7). The desire for new experiences should motivate pupils to seek the new joys of deeper godly living, through the strength of the Spirit. The need for achievement can be met by encouraging pupils to develop ideals and reach specific goals in Christian service and Christian living. The need for activity or expression challenges pupils to diligent service for the Lord in the local church and elsewhere.

Fifth, the Holy Spirit also grants Christian teachers the insight during lesson preparation to make them aware of pupil needs, and the insight during lesson presentation to help them make the pupils aware of their own needs.

Sixth, the Holy Spirit seeks to motivate pupils to learn by upholding before them ideals and goals in Christian living and service. The wise Christian teacher motivates learning by instilling ideals of conduct and by prompting the formulation of attainable goals. The New Testament contains numerous exhortations to Christians to achieve various goals.

Spirit-directed learning is the highest form of intrinsic motivation. In learning and appropriating divine truth, no motive can substitute for the pure inner urges implanted by God's Spirit. Pupils who are filled with the Spirit are supplied with the highest motives for Christian living and service. They desire to do "the will of God from the heart; with good will doing service, as unto the Lord, and not unto men" (Eph 6:6b-7). They desire to "learn to maintain good works" (Titus 3:14), to "seek the things that are above" (Col 3:1), and to "do all in the name of the Lord Jesus" (3:17).

Of course, only pupils who have been regenerated by God's Spirit through faith in Christ can enjoy full motivation for Christian living. Salvation brings "new motives which will be the power for breaking old habits and forming new ones."[2] The conversion experience, Edge points out, provides "the only adequate foundation and motivation for Christian living."[3] The unsaved pupil has little or no motivation for learning spiritual truth, till the Holy Spirit convinces him of sin and of his need of a Saviour. At that point, the one motivating factor present is the desire for possession of eternal life, acceptance with God, and a solution to sin in the life. At salvation, a person becomes a new creation in Christ (2 Co 5:17) with a new set of values and motives, waiting to be tapped and channeled by Spirit-led Christian teachers. Without Spirit-guided motivation, there is little or no pupil interest. And without interest, there is little or no Spirit-directed learning.

THE PRINCIPLE OF RELEVANCE

Relevance to life-needs is the second law or principle that governs effective learning. Not only must pupils be motivated to learn; they must also see how the truth to be learned relates to them personally.

Pupils tend to learn to the extent that lessons relate to their personal needs or problems. This law of learning is similar to, if not the same as, what some educators call the law of satisfaction. When spiritual needs are met, pupil interest is increased, learning is enhanced, and satisfaction results. Anderson quotes Hull as saying that "learning occurs because a need is satisfied either directly or indirectly."[4]

This principle of learning suggests to Christian teachers that they depend on the Spirit of God to enable them to: (1) introduce their lessons in ways that will capture interest and that will relate to the problems, needs, and experiences of pupils — as Christ often did; (2) show how the Bible is relevant to pupils' experiences; and (3) lead pupils to see and appropriate the Word of the Lord as the answer to their personal needs.

The importance of this principle of learning is well summarized by LeBar:

> If our pupils see no connection between their own needs and the Word, it may be spoken into the air in their vicinity, but will yield little fruit because it doesn't get inside. If it is associated with an interest, they will listen with attention which may lead to something deeper. If they see how the Bible meets a need, they will make some effort to find God's answer.[5]

THE PRINCIPLE OF ACTIVITY

The third principle of learning is also called the law of experience, practice, involvement, or interaction. Educators agree that the self-activity of pupils is basic to effective learning. Pupils learn to do by doing. The activity may be physical, mental, or emotional, but there must be activity if learning is to take place. Interestingly, the Greek word translated "to learn" is frequently used in the sense of learning or appropriating "to oneself less through instruction than through experience or practice."[6]

But how can learning be an active process if learning depends on the Holy Spirit? Doesn't the Spirit's presence in the learning process suggest that pupils need to rely only on Him, rather than on their participation or personal involvement? The answer to the second question is negative, because one thing the Spirit purposes to do in the learning process is to help pupils interact with what they have discovered in the Word so that they become more Christlike in their attitudes and actions. The Holy Spirit encourages pupil activity so that there will be interaction of the total personality — mind, emotion, and will — with God's Word. And He guides submissive teachers to assist their pupils in interacting with the right persons, the right things, and the right ideas, to the end that they may advance spiritually. Spirit-filled teachers are capable of being directed by the Spirit in choosing life-problems for their pupils to deal with, and issues for them to think about.

THE PRINCIPLE OF READINESS

Readiness, as a law of learning, is related to motivation, but is not identical with it. Motivation may be thought of as the stimulation of the desire to learn, whereas readiness may be thought of as the conditioning or preparedness for learning. Taken in this sense, motivation could be considered an aspect of readiness.

The law of readiness points to the fact that pupils learn more effectively when they are prepared to learn. Readiness stimulates thinking, provides a foundation on which teachers can build, excites interest in learning, creates greater anticipation for learning, and stimulates habits of independent study.

There are various means by which pupils may be made ready to learn. Activities such as reading, field trips, observation, interviews, thought-questions, and so on, enhance the readiness factor. Pupils are also ready to learn to the extent that they are conscious of their needs and are aided by proper home relationships and teacher relationships. Other factors that affect readiness are past experiences, social pressures, physical and mental development, awareness of spiritual deficiencies.

Does the Holy Spirit provide all pupils with equal readiness to learn? No, for several reasons:

First, God has a different plan or "divine time-table" for each pupil. In His sovereign grace, He has planned for some pupils to come to an understanding of certain truths more quickly than other pupils. Even in Christ's earthly ministry some were quicker to grasp His truth than others. The rate of spiritual growth for some pupils may be slower or faster at times than for others. Some students may be apathetic to learning the Bible because of sin or failure to respond to the Spirit's past teaching ministry. A Christian pupil is grieving the Spirit if he displays lack of interest in the truth. An unregenerate pupil may lack enthusiasm for the things of God simply because he is unsaved, and therefore is not indwelt by the Spirit (Ro 8:9; 1 Co 2:14).

Second, the personalities, mental capacities, and spiritual abilities of pupils differ. Rate of growth varies from pupil to pupil and is determined, in part, by heredity and environment.

Third, teachers may be responsible for the lack of readiness on the part of some pupils, because of poor teacher-pupil relationships, ignorance of pupils' needs, or lack of being properly adjusted to the Holy Spirit.

With reference to the law of readiness, the Holy Spirit works through the past experiences of pupils to bring them, in God's own time, to higher levels of spiritual living, and He conditions pupils' receptivity by making them aware of existing needs. He stimulates teachers to greater personal concern for their pupils. And He adjusts and arranges circumstances that will bring about learning.

This principle of learning suggests that Christian teachers teach those spiritual truths that their pupils are most capable of learning at that particular stage of their spiritual development. This principle also suggests that teachers look to the Holy Spirit to direct them in the choice of those teaching techniques that will best create pupil readiness. Because environment affects pupil readiness, teachers ought to arrange environmental factors so as to facilitiate maximum learning. This means being concerned about room appearance, furniture arrangement, room temperature, lighting, ventilation, adequate space, proper wall colors, room "decorations" (curtains, bulletin boards), and so on.

Since readiness involves the removal of hindrances to learning, it is imperative that teachers be aware of what these hindering factors are. Lack of motivation, lack of lesson preparation, failure to involve pupils in meaningful lesson activities, failure to relate Bible truths to life-needs — these are factors that hinder learning. Another factor is spiritual blindness or lack of salvation. Leading pupils to accept Christ as Saviour is the first step in giving them the readiness to comprehend Bible truths. Therefore the plan of salvation should be taught clearly and repeatedly.

Carnality or lack of yieldedness on the part of regenerate pupils also hinders learning. The main need of the learner who is a Christian is yieldedness or commitment. Trentham states that "obedience to the truth revealed to us is a spiritual condition upon which further revelations of truth depend."[7] The carnal believer (1 Co 3:1) is incapable of appropriating divine truth and is unable "to discern good and evil" (Heb 5:14). Chafer maintains that "there can be no full or worthy apprehension of God's revealed truth by the Christian who is unspiritual or carnal. Hence the imperative aspect of a yielded life."[8] To comprehend the revelation of the mind and will of God, believers must yield their lives to God and thus have their minds transformed by the power of God to recognize "the good and acceptable and perfect will of God" (Ro 12:1-2).

Pupils who understand the will of God are those who are filled with the Holy Spirit (Eph 5:17-18). Thus it may be concluded that the filling of the Spirit increases the capacity of pupils to learn more quickly and adequately. This does not suggest, however, that pupils' intelligence quotients or mental capacities are necessarily heightened by the Spirit's filling. Pupils are simply made more open or receptive to the Spirit's teaching ministry. The ability to learn spiritual truths increases in proportion to yieldedness to the Spirit of God. Prayer, spiritual preparation, and an obedient heart are also essential to genuine learning.

Does this emphasis, however, on learning principles and pupil experience nullify the work of the Spirit and suggest a return to the naturalistic educational philosophy of John Dewey? No, because the person who is teaching in light of these basic learning principles is really following the master Teacher, Jesus Christ — not John Dewey. Witmer addresses himself to this fact:

> Learning that takes place in life situations, that grows out of need, that is stimulated by interest, that is conceived as growth is as old as Christian education itself. The founder of Christianity Himself, the world's Master Teacher, practiced that kind of education.[9]

Concern for learning principles does not decimate the place of the Spirit's teaching ministry because the teaching of the

Holy Spirit is no substitute for learning, and learning takes place basically by means of the Holy Spirit. Therefore the prayer of each Christian pupil should be that of the psalmist: "Give me understanding, that I may learn thy commandments" (Ps 119:73).

13

Principles of Teaching and the Work of the Spirit

JUST AS THERE ARE CERTAIN basic factors that facilitate learning, so there are certain factors that govern effective teaching. Knowing the laws of teaching and how the Spirit of God works through those laws can greatly assist teachers in their ministry of declaring truth and guiding pupils. As Gregory illustrates, "He who would gain harvest must obey nature's laws for the growing of corn, and he who would teach a child successfully must follow the laws of teaching."[1]

The four principles of learning discussed in the preceding chapter relate specifically to activities involving the *learner*. If the learner is to learn most effectively, (1) he must be motivated; (2) he must have his needs met; (3) he must be actively involved; (4) he must be prepared.

The laws of teaching relate specifically to the self-activities of the *teacher*. Three of the more basic teaching "laws" are the principle of preparation, the principle of pupil understanding, and the principle of communication.

THE PRINCIPLE OF PREPARATION

Effective teaching begins with a prepared teacher — a prepared life, as well as a prepared lesson. To teach others,

Christian teachers must be in vital union with Christ, filled with the Word and the Spirit. Edge asserts that "the single most important factor that influences learning is the *life and personality of the teacher.*"[2] This is true, he points out, because (1) teaching techniques are of little use unless they are used by one through whose life the truth and love of God radiate; (2) Christian truths are better understood when seen in life; (3) lives are impressed and changed more by truths they see demonstrated than by those they merely hear spoken. For these reasons, Christian teachers should be selected with great care.

The learning of the Spirit certainly does not preclude study and preparation on the part of teachers. In fact, the better prepared the teachers are, the better the Holy Spirit can use them in class sessions. A creative teacher brings to his class a prepared heart, a knowledge of his subject, a conviction of the truths to be taught, and a desire to guide his students into the spiritual experiences he has enjoyed with the Lord.

The Principle of Pupil Understanding

Successful teaching depends not only on knowledge of one's Saviour and one's lessons, but also one's pupils. A personal interest in and an understanding and appreciation of each pupil's problems and needs contributes to a close personal relationship between teacher and pupil which, in turn, fosters learning. Knowing the backgrounds, interests, difficulties, ambitions, attitudes, needs and levels of maturity of individual pupils enables teachers to select the most appropriate methods and teaching procedures. And this allows the Spirit to work to greatest advantage.

The more intimately a teacher knows his pupils, the better equipped he is to meet their needs. As he comes to know and work with his pupils as individuals, the Christian teacher can more easily direct them, with the aid of the Holy Spirit, to solutions found in God's holy Word.

> Does the farmer's study and understanding of the earth make God unnecessary? Not at all. It is still God's seed. It is still God's earth. It is still His sun and rain. It is still He who germinates the seed and who gives the increase. The farmer just cooperates more intelligently with God and enables him to bring forth a greater fruitage.[3]

Because only the Holy Spirit knows what changes must be affected in learners' hearts, it is imperative that teachers look to Him for greater insight into human personality and individual needs.

THE PRINCIPLE OF COMMUNICATION

The effective teacher is the one who, under the guidance of God's Spirit, communicates the truth he knows to the pupils he knows. Communicating God's truth implies that teachers use words understood in the same way by pupils and the teachers, and that the unknown be taught or approached through truths already known. It implies that under the Spirit's direction, every means possible and necessary be used to convey truth, such as illustrations, visual aids, testing of learning, pupil participation, permissive atmosphere, removal of distractions, proper pace of teaching, and so on.

With regard to pace of teaching or the rate at which teachers attempt to communicate quantity of content, Doll offers this suggestion: "Rather than teaching too much at a time, which results in superficial teaching and learning, [teachers] should limit their subject matter, striving to make it as meaningful as possible."[4] How else can teachers do this except under the specific direction of the Holy Spirit?

Christian teachers should constantly endeavor to improve their spiritual relationship to the Holy Spirit, their means of lesson preparation, their understanding of their pupils, and their ways of communicating spiritual truth. If teachers consider their God-given task of Christian teaching as involving eternal issues, they will constantly strive to improve. "Since the Spirit is always our Teacher, it is imperative that we always remain teachable."[5] To the extent that the Spirit is allowed to work freely in teachers, the teaching-learning process is facilitated, and Christian education goals are attained.

14

Methods and Materials
and the Work of the Spirit

DOES THE USE of teaching methods and materials nullify and
outrule the work of the Holy Spirit? Can the Holy Spirit
work through curriculum materials, or should teachers simply teach "from the Bible"?

THE HOLY SPIRIT AND METHODS

Christian educators maintain that there is nothing inherently wrong with methodology. Methods are tools or ways of
teaching; they are links for uniting content and experience.
Methods are vehicles for bringing learners in vital contact
with Christ and the Word. Method and message go hand
in hand, as Bowman elucidates:

> Some may express impatience with materials or methods
> as if they were an inconsequential, take-it-or-leave-it mat-
> ter. But method and message go together. . . . Some may
> minimize techniques as ephemeral and unrelated to the time-
> less truths of religion. But the best we know about good
> methods traces back for its clues to the *way* the Great
> Teacher taught as well as to what He said.[1]

Methodology is not contrary to the working of the Spirit.
"Methodicalness involves a description of how the Spirit works

138

through the mind and how one may cooperate with the Spirit so that He may function freely."[2]

There are dangers, however, to avoid in the use of methodology. Methods tend to become looked on as ends in themselves. And some teachers tend to use methods as substitutes for effort or preparation on their part. There is also the lurking danger that methods may substitute for the prime authority of God's scriptural revelation. Bell writes,

> With the increased concern for the Sunday School, the scientific method of teaching . . . and with new concepts of communication, it becomes imperative that these and other advances of improvements be anchored to the divine revelation and not become a clever means of substituting human opinions for the clear affirmations of Scripture.[3]

There are many varied methods in use in Christian education circles today. There are storytelling, lectures, visual aids, discussions, questions and answers, quizzes, reports, buzz groups, role playing, dramatizations, panels, debates, projects, field trips, and problem-solving. In view of these and many other teaching approaches, the selection of methods is an important matter in Christian teaching. Consider the following tests in selecting a method: time (in preparing and using the method), age of pupils, purpose, ability or skill of the teacher, equipment and facilities, and lesson content. The best method for any given occasion is the one that accomplishes the best results in the best way.

A major task of the Spirit in Christian teaching is choosing, or guiding teachers in choosing, the appropriate method or methods for the occasion at hand. The real Guide in Christian education is God the Spirit, and the methods of education are those that He chooses to use. As teachers consciously depend on the Spirit in prayer, He will guide them in choosing appropriate teaching techniques.

Therefore it is evident that methodology and the Holy Spirit are not incompatible. He works *through* methods to bring about spiritual nurture. The creative use of a variety of methods facilitates learning, and thus fosters spiritual change and maturation.

THE HOLY SPIRIT AND PRINTED
CURRICULUM MATERIALS

Whereas some teachers prefer to discard curriculum materials and "just teach the Bible," most Christian educators recognize the inestimable value of printed materials as teaching aids. The effectiveness of the Spirit's ministry is increased as He works through prepared human instruments who are constantly sharpening their efficiency through the use of varied teaching tools, including printed materials. Good materials are certainly not incompatible with the Holy Spirit.

Through the proper use of curricular materials, teachers are better equipped to provide direction, continuity, and life-relatedness in their teaching. Printed materials can help teachers understand the content to be taught, as well as enhance their ability to communicate that content by means of creative methods suited specifically to the abilities and interests of the age-group being taught.

Of course, there are varying degrees of excellence and quality in printed materials. "What teachers should look for in printed manuals is the extent to which the writers help them apply Scriptural principles to the local situation," LeBar suggests.[4] The Holy Spirit is related to printed materials in three ways: He guides writers and editors in the formulation of materials, He guides church leaders in the selection of materials, and He guides teachers in the use of materials — but only, of course, as those writers, editors, church leaders, and teachers rely on Him for His filling and guidance. Writers of curriculum materials should seek the guidance of the Holy Spirit as they structure and write curriculum series that aim to meet the highest scriptural and educational standards. Their ministry is strategic because it involves the planning of content sequence and methodology procedures which affect thousands of lives — teachers and pupils alike.

Church leaders should seek the guidance of the Spirit in selecting printed materials. Criteria for selecting material should include at least the following:

> (1) Is the material in harmony with the objective sought? (2) Is it true to the Bible? (3) Does it contain subversive doctrinal or social views? (4) Is it prepared by scholarly and otherwise capable writers? (5) Is it suited to the needs and capacities of the pupils? (6) Can the teachers use it successfully? (7) Is it otherwise practical in the light of local conditions?[5]

Of course, curriculum materials must be adapted to local conditions. Teachers must adjust the materials to meet needs, and this too calls for the Spirit's guidance.

As teachers read their manuals, they should evaluate the suggestions in terms of their own classes or groups. LeBar suggests that teachers ask the following questions as they adapt materials in lesson preparation:

> Does the spirit of the whole meet the needs of my pupils? Should they be different people after studying these lessons? Do the aims seem to be pointed directly at them — deeply, personally? Would a slight change of focus do more for them? Is each lesson needed by them, or is there one aspect of the whole that is most urgently needed? Can I strengthen this emphasis without destroying the continuity of the series? Might it be wise to revamp a lesson or two in order to stress the needed emphasis?[6]

These questions can best be answered as teachers rely on the Spirit of God in this preparatory step of teaching. Teachers will be better equipped to be led by the Spirit in adapting curriculum materials during the teaching process, if they have already relied on Him in the study of materials written under the Spirit's guidance and selected under the Spirit's leadership. Thus they will be more capable instruments in making God's written revelation understood and experienced by their pupils.

With the dynamic power of God's Holy Spirit working within Christian teachers, on or within pupils, through creative methods and materials, to exalt Christ through His written Word, Christian education is a thrilling spiritual adventure. "What a crime for any session to be dull when it ought to be positively exciting, prosaic when it ought to be dynamic, boring when it ought to be a great adventure!"[7] The teaching-learning process can be spiritually dynamic and fruitful as Christian teachers cooperate with the blessed Holy Spirit in the glorious and rewarding ministry of Christian education!

Part 5

A BRIEF HISTORY OF THE
HOLY SPIRIT IN TEACHING

What place have leaders in church history attributed to the Holy Spirit in teaching? How do the religious circumstances of the times affect the doctrine of the Spirit's teaching ministry? To what extent have Christians in the past utilized, in their teaching, the Holy Spirit's power for illumination, direction, and enablement?

This section is not intended as a survey of pneumatology (the doctrine of the Holy Spirit) nor as a history of Christian education. It is simply a summary of one aspect of the history of the doctrine of the Holy Spirit: His work as Teacher. Selected highlights from the early church period to modern times are discussed briefly.

15

The Holy Spirit and Teaching
Before the Reformation

THE ANTE-NICENE PERIOD

NOT TOO MUCH REFERENCE to the Holy Spirit's ministry as a Teacher is to be expected in the first few centuries of the church. Prior to the Council of Nicaea (A.D. 325), references to the Holy Spirit made in writing were made primarily in connection with the practical concerns of Christian experience more than with doctrines. Concerning the sub-apostolic writers of the first century and a half, Swete writes:

> There was as yet no formal theology of the Spirit and no effort to create it; nor was there any conscious heresy. But the presence of the Spirit in the Body of Christ was recognized on all hands as an acknowledged fact of the Christian life.[1]

Attention was directed mainly to the person of Christ in early controversial issues. When controversy concerning the Holy Spirit did arise (as the result of the presence of heresy), it dealt with His deity. The Apostles' Creed, early hymns and liturgies, and direct statements of early church fathers, such as Ignatius, Clement of Rome, Justin Martyr, Irenaeus, Clement of Alexandria, and Tertullian, affirm the general acceptance of the deity and personality of the Spirit. The early

145

church also referred (in passing comments, more than in formal statements) to the authorship of the Scriptures, regeneration, sanctification, and the future resurrection as works of the Holy Spirit.[2] He is also recognized as the source of Christian knowledge.

The apocryphal *Shepherd of Hermas,* with its numerous references to the Spirit of God, is perhaps one of the earliest writings to speak of the Spirit's teaching ministry. "Hermas speaks also of the Holy Spirit as the Teacher and Sanctifier of believers in general."[3]

In his *Dialogue with Trypho,* Justin Martyr, an apologist writing in defense of Christianity, replies to Plato's belief that God can be known by the mind by asking the questions, "Is there then in our minds a power such as this and so great? Will the human intellect ever see God unless it is furnished with the Holy Spirit?"[4] In the same work Justin Martyr states that believers

> receive, each one of them, gifts, according to their meetness, being illuminated through the name of this same Christ; for one receives the Spirit of understanding, and another the Spirit of counsel or strength or healing or foresight or teaching or of the fear of God.[5]

An interesting sidelight in Gnostic heresy was the belief held by some of Marcion's followers that the "other Paraclete" (Jn 14:16) was the apostle Paul!

One of the early references to the teaching work of the Spirit came because of the rise of the heresy of Montanism. Montanus and his followers held that they were the recipients of special revelation from the Spirit, who gave men truths in prophetic visions. Tertullian, who was a Montanist, was chiefly concerned, however, with the *teaching* work of the Spirit. He writes:

> The Paraclete, having many things to teach which the Lord reserved for Him . . . will first bear witness to Christ Himself . . . and glory Him and bring Him to our re-

membrance; and . . . He will proceed to reveal many things which appertain to the conduct of life.[6]

In his *Setting Forth of the Apostolic Preaching,* Irenaeus points out that it is through the Spirit that "the prophets prophesied, and the fathers learned the things of God, and the righteous were guided into the way of righteousness."[7]

Novatian's excellent tract on the Trinity refers to the Spirit as the Teacher of truth and Bestower of all spiritual gifts.[8]

Origen states that the Spirit enables men to acquire the gifts of learning, wisdom, and knowledge.[9]

That believers in the early church relied on the Spirit's teaching is evident from these writers who commented on the Spirit's work as an accepted factor in the devotional life of the church.

THE NICENE AND POST-NICENE PERIODS

The most significant doctrinal controversy of the early church revolved around Arius, who held that the Son and the Holy Spirit were created, and Athanasius, who affirmed their deity. The controversy was climaxed at the Nicene Council in 325 when Arius was denounced and the phrase, "I believe in the Holy Spirit," was stated in the Nicene Creed.

It is interesting that following this heated conflict, the Arian leaders called attention to the teaching and sanctifying work of the Spirit. The second Sirmian Creed (357), for example, reads: "The Paraclete Spirit is through the Son, who was sent and came according to promise to instruct, teach, and sanctify the Apostles and all believers."[10] Eunomius, an Arian, denied the deity and creative power of the Spirit, but believed in His sanctifying and enlightening power.[11]

The Council at Constantinople (381) added to the Nicene Creed a statement on the procession of the Spirit from the Father. This was the result of an outburst of semi-Arian "Macedonians," who were attacked by the Cappadocians, Basil of Caesarea, Gregory Nazianzen, and Gregory of Nyssa.

Basil, in writing about the Holy Spirit, declares that He illuminates, gives men foreknowledge, the understanding of
mysteries, a share in spiritual gifts, and so on.

Frequent reference is made in the post-Nicene period to
the Spirit's illuminating work. Athanasius refers to the Spirit
as the illuminating living Energy and Gift of the Son.[12] Cyril
of Jerusalem frequently makes mention of the Spirit as Illumi-
nator of the mind and soul in his *Catechetical and Mystogogic
Lectures*. "He enlightens the soul and makes it see what is
beyond human sight."[13] Theodoret says that we see the rays
of light which stream from the Son only as we are enlightened
by the Spirit. Without the Holy Spirit, according to Hilary
of Poitiers, man would be unable to apprehend God and would
even be destitute of the light of knowledge. Augustine makes
this statement regarding knowledge and the Spirit:

> A man could not have wisdom, understanding, counsel,
> courage, knowledge, godliness, and the fear of God, unless
> he had received the Spirit of wisdom, understanding, coun-
> sel, courage, knowledge, godliness, and the fear of God.[14]

Gregory the Great, in writing of the power of the Spirit to
make a fisherman a preacher (Peter), a persecutor a teacher
(Paul), and a publican an evangelist (Matthew), states these
interesting words:

> Men are drawn to whatever the Spirit wills. They have no
> need to learn their new calling; as soon as He touches the
> mind, He teaches it. The mind of man is changed im-
> mediately as it falls under His enlightenment.[15]

The Council of Toledo (589) added the "filioque" phrase
("and the Son") to the creeds of Nicaea and Constantinople,
indicating that the Western Church believed in the procession of the Spirit from both the Father and the Son. The
Greek Church did not accept this inclusion, and this difference
was one of the major causes for the division of the East and
West in 1054. "After the decline of this controversy the his-

tory of the doctrine is concernd chiefly with the work of the Holy Spirit rather than His Person."[16]

The Augustinian-Pelagian controversy has little bearing on the Spirit's task of teaching the believer, because its chief debate was over Augustine's emphasis on the efficacious grace of the Holy Spirit versus Pelagius' view of the natural goodness of men without any need for the Spirit's redemptive work. However, Augustine, in his *De Magistro* on epistemology and education, insists that man possesses an innate capacity for truth.[17] Augustine said that the real Teacher of the Christian is the indwelling Christ. Grimes makes this summary regarding Augustine's view of learning:

> One does not learn religious truth through its being "poured in," as it were, from the outside; rather it is learned in the fullest sense only when it is a matter of inner apprehension.[18]

THE MIDDLE AGES

The hierarchical developments within the church in the Middle Ages led to a recognition, by many, of the Roman Catholic church as the authority in spiritual matters. The Roman church taught that it is the custodian and interpreter of the Scriptures. So conceived, the Scriptures were without the need of the Holy Spirit's illuminating work; and Christians were to be taught, if taught at all, by the church, not the Holy Spirit. "It was expressly denied that the Spirit could teach all Christians through the Word of God. Earthly priests were substituted for the Holy Spirit."[19]

The acceptance of doctrine on the basis of creedal statement, rather than on the basis of the written Word of God, led to cold formalism and tradition. This tended to stifle any flicker of vital interest in the Holy Spirit and His work. Intellectual and spiritual darkness prevailed. This led to moral poverty and corruption and thus to a virtual indifference to the things of the Spirit of God.

The powerlessness of the organized church led those interested in spiritual virility to the excesses of mysticism. With its stress on direct, personal contact with God, mysticism naturally stressed the Holy Spirit's direct illumination on the mind and soul. Some well-known medieval mystics were St. Bernard of Clairvaux, Hugo of St. Victor, Hildegard, Joachim, Occam, Eckhart, Suso, Tauler, and Ruysbroeck. The Albigenses and Cathari were groups of believers concerned with mysticism and the spiritual life.

Counteracting these mystical elements was Scholasticism, with its rationalistic approach which obstructed interest in the Holy Spirit. Duns Scotus, Albertus Magnus, and Thomas Aquinas were representative figures. It is interesting that, according to Rees, "Aquinas treats the whole subject of revelation without referring to the Spirit."[20] Aquinas wrote this about God as Teacher: "Just as a doctor, although he works exteriorly while nature alone works interiorly, is said to cause healing, so man is said to teach, although he announces exteriorly while God teaches interiorly."[21]

The failure of the Crusades dulled spiritual zeal, and philosophical interests squelched a concern for the inner teaching ministry of the Holy Spirit.

16

The Holy Spirit and Teaching from the Reformation to the Present

THE PROTESTANT REFORMATION

"THE PERIOD OF THE REFORMATION . . . gave a testimony to the Holy Spirit more full and explicit than had ever been uttered since the apostolic age."[1] The sovereignty of God, depravity of man, the authority of the Bible, efficacious grace, and justification by faith were doctrines emphasized in the Reformation.

Reformers were concerned with the work of the Holy Spirit in relation to four specific areas: regeneration, illumination, the Scriptures, and the sacraments. The Reformers taught that regeneration comes by the efficacious grace of God's Spirit, not through the church. In place of the priestly sacerdotalism of the Roman Catholic church, the doctrine of the priesthood of all believers (the right to read and interpret the Scriptures individually and privately) was taught by the Reformers.

According to the Reformers, the Holy Spirit in illumination opens the minds and hearts of believers to receive the Word of God. Sometimes the ministry of illumination seemed to be considered a part of regeneration. Calvin says, "By His Spirit illuminating their minds and forming their hearts to the love and cultivation of righteousness, He makes them new creatures."[2]

The Helvetic Confession, a post-Reformation creed, indicates a similar teaching:

> In regeneration the understanding is enlightened by the Holy Spirit to understand both the mysteries and the will of God, and the will itself is not only charged by the Spirit, but also furnished with powers both to will and to do good spontaneously (Ro 8:5-6).[3]

Luther and Calvin both had much to say concerning the Holy Spirit's relation to the Bible. Luther strongly opposed the "enthusiasts" or "spiritualists" of his day (of whom Carlstadt was a leading proponent), who taught that the Spirit works apart from or beyond the Scriptures. Prenter has written an entire book describing Luther's controversy with the enthusiasts.[4] Luther taught that the Spirit and the Word are so intimately joined that the Spirit never goes beyond the written Word.

Calvin taught that the Word of God has "no efficacy unless at the same time the Holy Spirit works in the hearts of the hearers, creating faith and making men's minds open to receive the Word."[5] Calvin did not teach that the Spirit causes Scripture to *become* the Word of God, as Niesel, a neoorthodox interpreter of Calvin, seems to say.[6] Instead, Calvin taught that the Holy Spirit testifies to the heart of believers that the objective body of truth is of divine origin and authoritatively true.

The Holy Spirit, Calvin affirms, works alongside of the written Word and not apart from it. "It is no less reasonable to boast of the Spirit without the Word, than it would be an absurd thing to bring forward the Word without the Spirit."[7]

Whereas Luther taught that the Spirit cannot make Christ real without the preceding ministry of the preached word, Calvin held that the Spirit can illuminate "in an internal manner . . . without the intervention of any preaching."[8] Both men, of course, agreed that the Spirit works through the written Word, never apart from it and never beyond it.

It is obvious from this brief survey of the Reformers' views on the teaching work of the Holy Spirit that "the developed doctrine of the work of the Holy Spirit is an exclusively Reformation doctrine."[9]

THE POST-REFORMATION PERIOD

The Reformation had freed many people from the bondage of Roman Catholicism. However, the Reformation, along with the intellectual and cultural interests of the Renaissance (which had been catalyzed by the expanding influence of the Crusades, the universities, and commerce), gave rise to the excesses of independent thinking in the seventeenth and eighteenth centuries. Man's accomplishments led him to place undue confidence in himself and his abilities. This found its peak of expression in subjectivism — the attitude that places authority in human religious feeling (mystical or emotional subjectivism) or in human reason (rationalistic subjectivism). The former type of subjectivism sometimes appealed to the Holy Spirit apart from the Scriptures; the latter rejected both the Spirit and the Scriptures.

The Puritan movement in England stressed the need for holy living through the direct teaching work of the Spirit, which was associated with the intuitive perceptions of the soul. The place of intuitive immediacy led to an attitude of disdain toward reasoning, study, and education. The Puritans believed that they could be taught by the Holy Spirit directly, apart from intermediary helps such as human teachers, methods, books, or even the Bible.[10]

Rationalism took the form of deism in England, skepticism in Germany, and atheism in France. It was within this intellectual soil that the roots of philosophic rationalism were planted and blossomed later in the nineteenth century in the form of liberalistic theology. Obviously, the work of the Spirit as a Teacher was entirely neglected in this intellectual climate.

Reaction to Puritanism led to ecclesiasticism in the Church of England, which, in turn, was met with the protest of Quakerism against cold sacramentalism and formal religion. With their emphasis on the Holy Spirit as the "inner light" of the soul, the Quakers, like the Puritans, admitted no need for the Scriptures. Robert Barclay, a disciple of George Fox, wrote that "the testimony of the Spirit is that alone by which the true knowledge of God hath been, is, and can be only revealed."[11] Along with the Quakers' claim to the "immediate consciousness" of the Spirit's revealing work came extravagant claims to "immediate leadings" by the Spirit in everyday activities.

Pietism in Germany shared some similar convictions. Jacob Boehme, a leading Pietist, professed a unique spiritual insight into divine mysteries. According to him, those who possess this illumination and are therefore children of light, have within them the Holy Spirit moving and reigning and teaching them all things.[12]

The revival movement under Wesley and Whitefield in England and America restored a needed emphasis on regeneration by the Spirit. Wesley taught the necessity of the Spirit for holy living and for guidance into all truth.

MODERN TIMES

In the nineteenth and twentieth centuries, the doctrine of the teaching ministry of the Spirit has been treated variously. Schleiermacher's "religion of feeling" denied the personality of the Spirit. This restoration of the heresy of Sabellianism had no place for the Spirit as Teacher. And the theory of Ritschl lacked any significant and pure presentation of the doctrine of the Holy Spirit.

In the nineteenth century the theological world was greatly influenced by German rationalistic philosophy, the evolutionary theory, higher criticism of the Bible, and optimistic post-millennialism. Tenets of liberal theology, including the denial of the personality of the Spirit, were widely adhered to. Revivalism under the leadership of Edwards, Finney, Moody, and others, stressed the power of the Spirit in salvation; but this did comparatively little to help believers formulate a clear concept of the Holy Spirit as the Teacher of divine truth in Christian hearts. Evangelism was stressed far more than education or edification, though the presence of converts provided a situation ripe for a work of education.

The twentieth century is marked with interesting developments in the study of the relationship of the Holy Spirit to Christian education.

Basically, four theological positions are dominating the American "Christian" scene in the twentieth century, each of which has had direct bearing on religious education. They are liberalism, neoorthodoxy, neoliberalism, and Evangelicalism.

The teaching of old liberalism, which had its heyday in the first three decades of the century, included an optimistic belief in the goodness of man, a utopian outlook toward human society, an emphasis on the immanence of God with little stress on His transcendence, a rejection of the finality of biblical revelation, and an acceptance of a unitarian concept of Jesus Christ. All of this, as can easily be seen, left no place for the work of the Holy Spirit in regeneration or Christian experience. A rejection of the deity of Jesus Christ and a concern for divine immanence meant a virtual dismissal of a belief in the Trinity, with an accompanying disregard for the Holy Spirit as the divine Teacher, possessing full deity and personality, operative in the hearts of men to redeem and instruct.

Liberal religious educators shared the same doctrinal viewpoints. Progressive religious education began to thrive in that very theological atmosphere, along with the endorsement of Dewey's empirical approach to education.

A belief in man's essential goodness led educators to more interest in pupils' growth patterns and human development than in content to be taught. An optimistic view toward society meant that religious education became socially organized and that social values were regarded more highly than spiritual values. The belief in divine immanence resulted in a blurring of distinctions between the operations of the human and divine elements in Christian education.

George Albert Coe, the foremost spokesman of liberal religious education in the early twentieth century and an able theorist of progressive religious education, did much to plant the experience-centered approach of Dewey into religious education. Coe may well be called "the John Dewey of religious education," though immanence rather than naturalism was his basic religious principle. While Dewey taught that learning is the continuous reconstruction of experience, Coe was saying that "continuous reconstruction is . . . the essence of the divine work in and through the human."[13]

Such an outlook toward religious education involved a repudiation of the Spirit's teaching ministry on three counts.

First, the denial of original sin and the avowal of the goodness of man's nature meant that character could be produced by proper environmental influences which, in turn, dissipated altogether any need for supernatural instruction.

Gaebelein aptly describes this weakness:

> The fatal error of Protestant liberalism in dealing with character education lies in its substitution of an adequate psychological method for the work of the Holy Spirit. Only the Spirit of God can make Christians. And He does it through His sovereign use of the truth set forth in Scripture.[14]

Second, the methodology of progressive religious education repudiated the need for the supernatural teaching of the Spirit. Experience-centered education emphasized progressive growth and questioned the necessity of the Holy Spirit's redemptive work.

Third, an inadequate view of values left the teacher with no absolute realities to teach. The only concern of the religious liberal educator was to reconstruct religion by releasing the creative religious experiences of the pupils. Adhering to Dewey's principle of relative values caused religious educators to reject the Christian view of the finality of biblical revelation.

The second major theological position is neoorthodoxy. Smart, a neoorthodox religious educator, describes the situation which gave birth to its exposure in America:

> Liberal optimism about human nature was shattered by the outbreak of startling forms of inhumanity within Western civilization. Modern man, confronted by evil in its naked reality, began to find the Biblical description of it once more believable. The idea of an inevitable progress of the human race no longer carried conviction, and the corollary belief, that divinity is to be identified with the natural process by which man moves toward the fulfillment of his destiny, seemed hard to distinguish from a humanism in which all belief in God is abandoned. The bankruptcy of unreconstructed liberalism was impossible to conceal, and the exposure was helped forward by theologians such as Barth and Brunner in Europe, and Reinhold Niebuhr in America.[15]

When the utopian hopes of liberalism were shattered by two world wars, neoorthodoxy found a solid footing in American theological soil. But what did it teach concerning the Holy Spirit? And how has religious education reacted to it as a theological movement?

Neoorthodoxy has restored an emphasis on the utter desperation of man's depraved nature, the absolute "otherness" of God's sovereign transcendence, and the centrality of revelation. However, it is still far from orthodox Evangelicalism. The Bible, says the neoorthodox theologian, is not to be equated with the Word of God. The Bible merely *contains* the Word of God, and is a record of past revelation. It is a human book, containing errors, and becomes the Word of God only when it speaks personally to its readers. According to neoorthodoxy, God's revelation is His supernatural breaking into history through man's personal encounter with Jesus Christ. The Holy Spirit is the existential, subjective operation of God, making His revelation become truth to man.[16] The Spirit prepares man for receiving the revelation of God.

Emil Brunner is in direct conflict with liberal religious education when he states that the life of faith does not belong to the sphere of education, but is higher than education. Elliott writes that, according to Brunner, "The Christian faith is not something which has been discovered by human instrumentalities nor can the Christian faith be interpreted through educational processes."[17] Education does have a place, according to Brunner, but a minor one. It is the "human carrier for the proclamation of the 'Word of God.' "[18]

> But the understanding and acceptance of the divine revelation to the Christian experience which is thus made possible are not dependent upon such an educational process. Indeed, what is happening in the experience of the individuals who have the "Word" proclaimed to them through an educational process is in an entirely different and separate realm.[19]

The quasimodalistic view of the Trinity and the subjective reception of revelation, along with a disparaging of human capabilities, make neoorthodoxy a system that has little to voice regarding the human and divine elements in Christian teaching.

Liberal religious educators reacted strongly against the inroads of this "new theology." Coe was one of the first to write against it.[20] Elliott's book, *Can Religious Education Be Christian?*, is a strong effort to defend and expound liberal, progressive religious education against neoorthodoxy.

In recent years, more and more religious educators have espoused neoorthodoxy as their theological frame of reference. In fact, Little refers to neoorthodox Christian education as "the new philosophy of Christian education."[21] This position is represented by educators such as Iris V. Cully, James D. Smart, and D. Campbell Wyckoff. They have placed an emphasis on the Bible in teaching but still maintain the erroneous neoorthodox view toward the Bible.*

The third major theological platform in the twentieth century is neoliberalism. Neoorthodoxy so undermined the foundational tenets of "old" liberalism that many liberals have reconstructed their theology into what is called neoliberalism. The classic work representing such a move among liberal educators was H. Shelton Smith's *Faith and Nurture,* written in 1941, in which his purpose was to "reconstruct . . . theological foundations in light of more realistic insights of current Christian faith."[22] Neoliberals stress the greatness and grace of God, the dual nature of man as a child of God and a fallen creature, the centrality of revelation, and the reconciling work of Christ.[23] Many refer to the Holy Spirit as the "agent" operative in the church.

The fourth theological platform of twentieth-century America is Evangelicalism. In the first several decades of this century, Evangelicals were staunch in their defence of orthodox truths against the insipid doctrines of liberalism. Accordingly, doctrinal rectitude was stressed, and Bible teachers were concerned primarily with transmitting scriptural truth.

Liberals reacted against this emphasis on content, because to them it spelled sterile orthodoxy and routine transmission of content. But they did not turn to the better. They placed the pupil and his experiences, instead of the Word of God, at the center of the educational orbit. Thus this liberal emphasis, just as much as so-called transmissivism, failed to see the need for the dynamic spiritual power of the Holy Spirit, energizing every phase of the teaching-learning process.

*See chapter 8 for a critique of neoorthodox Christian education.

Today, most evangelical Christian educators are seeing the need for giving due regard to both biblical content *and* the Holy Spirit's ministry in the educational process. To Evangelicals, the Bible is the basic content to be transmitted in Christian education, but God's Spirit provides the spiritual power so essential for communicating His truth effectively.

Summary: Go . . . Teach

ONCE A TEACHER recognizes that the work of God the Holy Spirit is indispensable in the teaching-learning process, teaching takes on exciting dimensions.

Following are five implications stemming from, or summarizing, this study.

1. REMEMBER THAT CHRISTIAN EDUCATION IS A SUPERNATURAL TASK

The presence of God's Holy Spirit in teaching takes Christian education beyond mere programming, methodology, and techniques. The Spirit's work in education makes it a divine, supernatural ministry.

Christian education takes on new perspective when viewed as God's work, not man's, as the energy of the Spirit, not of the flesh. Seen as a divine work, teaching God's truths becomes a responsibility of fantastic proportions and implications. As you acknowledge the work of the Spirit, you see that Christian education involves high objectives, a holy Book, divine truth, eternal souls, heavenly issues, and a divine, infallible Teacher. As LeBar has aptly stated,

> How superlative ought to be any form of Christian teaching, with so many supernatural distinctives — the infallible written Word revealing our Creator-Redeemer God who

161

sent His Son to be King of kings, and the Holy Spirit working within the teacher, upon or within the pupil, to exalt the Saviour through the inscripturated record![1]

Chafer eloquently discusses two reasons why the Spirit's teaching is supernaturally sublime:

> There is no didactic discipline in the world comparable to the teaching of Christ by the Holy Spirit, both because of the fact that infinity characterizes the themes which are taught, and because of the Teacher's method of approach by which He, by the Spirit, enters the innermost recesses of the heart where impressions originate and there not only tells out the truth of transcendent magnitude, but causes the pupil actually to grasp the things thus revealed. "By faith we understand" (Heb 11:3). That Christ would continue the teaching begun while here on earth was clearly promised (John 16:12-15), and implied in Acts 1:1 where reference is made to "all that Jesus began both to do and to teach."[2]

2. RELY ON THE HOLY SPIRIT

Teachers are effective only to the extent that they rely on, and are yielded to, the Holy Spirit. Though Christian education is a divine task, it is also a process involving humans, a process in which teachers must cooperate *with* God, rather than work against Him. Seen in the light of the Spirit's teaching ministry, Christian education suggests that teachers be submissive to the Spirit in lesson preparation and be ready for His guidance during class sessions. LeBar forcefully depicts the matter of yieldedness to the Spirit:

> Only a tool, only a channel are we in the hands of God. Yes, in one sense; yet both these figures are inadequate because tools and channels are dead and mechanical while human instruments have wills of their own. The Lord does not purpose to deaden our wills or render them mechanical, but to activate them under His control. He does not propose to break our wills, for we shall need the full force of

them in our struggle against evil. He wants us deliberately to identify our wills with His.

This will mean the total submission of the old self-life with its longings and strivings. This means that we shall be constantly looking to Him rather than around us, constantly listening to Him when it is more natural to talk, constantly obeying His slightest indication without question.[3]

The need for dependence on the Spirit of God is one factor that makes Christian education distinct from secular education. According to Bell, "It is the need for supernatural help that places both teacher and pupil in a position unknown in the secular field."[4]

3. RELATE GOD'S WORD TO PUPIL'S EXPERIENCES

The Holy Spirit has given God's holy Word — the content of Christian education — but, in addition, is concerned that the propositional truths of God's written revelation become personally appropriated by the students. A proper understanding of the educational work of the Holy Spirit provides Christian teachers with a balanced, blended approach to the question of content and experience. Only by the Holy Spirit is subject matter transmitted to the experiences of the pupils, the outer Word made a part of inner experience, and propositional truths made personal.[5]

4. REST SATISFIED WITH NOTHING LESS THAN SPIRITUAL RESULTS

The goals of teaching, as suggested by the biblical doctrine on the Spirit's teaching, are more than the acquisition of knowledge, the establishment of educational programs, or the utilization of effective techniques. As a divine task of God's Spirit, Christian education is the impartation of the truth of God to secure pupil's wholehearted conformity to God's will.

Effective teachers evaluate what results they are or are not gaining, and strive to see spiritual results — that is, results of the Spirit — accomplished. They ask themselves, What kind of results am I working for in my teaching? What kind of results am I getting? Teachers cannot assume that they are automatically getting spiritual results. They must constantly test their teaching, at the same time depending on the Spirit for spiritual fruit.

5. RECOGNIZE THAT, IN THE FINAL SENSE, GOD THE HOLY SPIRIT IS THE TEACHER

It is God who does the teaching. The Bible teacher is a channel of His grace, an instrument doing the planting and watering. The increase is from God (1 Co 3:6). The spiritual effectiveness of Christian teaching rests ultimately with God the Spirit. Every Christian teacher and pupil ought to pray in the words of David, "Teach me thy way, O Jehovah" (Ps 27:11). Before God can teach pupils through a teacher, that teacher must first be taught by Him. Then with the psalmist he can say, "Thou hast taught me" (Ps 119:102). (Other verses that speak of God as Teacher are Ps 71:17, 86:11, 94:12; Is 28:26, 48:17.) Job triumphantly exalts God as Teacher by the rhetorical question, "Who is a teacher like unto him?" (Job 36:22).

The dynamic work of the Holy Spirit in teaching is what makes Christian education a glorious work. This is what makes the teaching of God's holy truths a noble, and at the same time enjoyable, task.

"Go . . . teach!"

Those are the compelling words of our resurrected Lord (Mt 28:19, KJV). Words that call for missionary sacrifice. Words that call for willing obedient service. But words that also call for dedication to an *educational* ministry.

Go teach *confidently,* in the power of the Holy Spirit, your Teacher.

Go teach *joyously,* in the realization that you are in partnership with the blessed Holy Spirit in a divine-human process.

Go teach *purposefully,* with the goal of spiritual transformation, growth, and change before you.

Go teach *creatively,* aware of the laws of teaching and learning, the principles by which God the Spirit helps pupils learn.

Go teach *reverently,* with gratitude that you are privileged to handle and communicate God's inspired, authoritative Word.

Go teach *convincingly,* with the assurance that you are engaged in the greatest task in the world: introducing others to the written Word and the living Word, God's Book, and God's Son!

Notes

Introduction

1. Lois E. LeBar, *Education That Is Christian*, p. 15.
2. Carl F. H. Henry, "Divine Revelation and the Bible," *Inspiration and Interpretation*, p. 256.
3. Ibid., p. 257.
4. Andrew Murray, *The Spirit of Christ: Thoughts on the Indwelling of the Holy Spirit in the Believer and the Church*, p. 219.
5. James DeForest Murch, *Christian Education and the Local Church*, pp. 155-56.
6. J. Theodore Mueller, "The Holy Spirit and the Scriptures," *Revelation and the Bible*, p. 276.
7. Charles Hodge, *Systematic Theology*, 3:472-73.
8. Ronald S. Wallace, *Calvin's Doctrine of the Word and Sacrament*, pp. 128-29.
9. Ibid., p. 128, citing Calvin's commentary on Luke 24:45.

PART 1

Chapter 1

1. W. E. Biederwolf, *Help to the Study of the Holy Spirit*, p. 17.
2. Franz Delitzsch, *Biblical Commentary on the Prophecies of Isaiah*, 1: 282.
3. Brooke Foss Westcott, *The Gospel According to St. John: The Authorised Version with Introduction and Notes*, p. 230; Hart, *Hulsean Lectures*, pp. 57-59, cited by Henry Barclay Swete, *The Holy Spirit in the New Testament*, p. 155; and John Charles Ryle, *Expository Thoughts on John*, 3:82.
4. John Peter Lange, "John," in *Lange's Commentary on the Holy Scriptures*, p. 442.
5. Westcott, p. 212.
6. E. Y. Mullins, "Paraclete," *International Standard Bible Encyclopedia*, 4:2245.
7. Westcott, p. 213; Hermann Cremer, *Biblico-Theological Lexicon of New Testament Greek*, p. 338; and R. C. H. Lenski, *The Interpretation of St. John's Gospel*, p. 998.
8. Julius Charles Hare, *The Mission of the Comforter*, p. 309.
9. Clement Clemance, *The Scripture Doctrine of the Holy Spirit*, p. 42.
10. S. D. F. Salmond, "The Epistle to the Ephesians," in *The Expositor's Greek Testament*, 3:273-74.

Chapter 2

1. Lewis Sperry Chafer, *He That Is Spiritual,* p. 62.
2. G. G. Findlay, "St. Paul's First Epistle to the Corinthians," *The Expositor's Greek Testament,* 2:784.
3. Henry Barclay Swete, *The Holy Spirit in the New Testament,* p. 153.
4. Archibald Thomas Robertson, *Word Pictures in the New Testament,* 4:89.
5. Albert Barnes, *Notes on the New Testament Explanatory and Practical, Luke and John,* p. 348; Marcus Dods, "The Gospel of St. John," *The Expositor's Greek Testament,* 1:835.
6. John F. Walvoord, "How Can Man Know God?" *Bibliotheca Sacra,* 116:106-7, April-June, 1959.

Chapter 3

1. J. I. Packer, *"Fundamentalism" and the Word of God,* pp. 111-12.
2. Henry Wheeler Robinson, *The Christian Experience of the Holy Spirit,* p. 182.
3. L. Gaussen, *The Inspiration of the Holy Scriptures,* pp. 118-23.
4. William F. Arndt and F. Wilbur Gingrich, *A Greek-English Lexicon of the New Testament and Other Early Christian Literature,* p. 248.
5. Julius Charles Hare, *The Mission of the Comforter,* pp. 348-55 (Note K).
6. For example, John F. Walvoord, *The Holy Spirit,* pp. 112-14.
7. Lewis Sperry Chafer, *Systematic Theology,* 3:322.
8. Kenneth S. Wuest, *The Practical Use of the Greek New Testament,* p. 152.
9. A. Plummer, *The Epistles of St. John, with Notes, Introduction and Appendices,* p. 61.
10. Abraham Kuyper, *The Work of the Holy Spirit,* p. 185.
11. Archibald Thomas Robertson, *Word Pictures in the New Testament,* 6:218.
12. R. C. H. Lenski, *The Interpretation of the Epistles of St. Peter, St. John and St. Jude,* p. 442.
13. Henry Alford, *The Greek Testament,* 4:455.
14. Kenneth S. Wuest, *In These Last Days,* p. 138.
15. Albert Benjamin Simpson, *The Holy Spirit,* 2:324-25.
16. Joseph Henry Thayer, *A Greek-English Lexicon of the New Testament,* p. 663.
17. John Calvin, *Institutes of the Christian Religion,* 1:638 (Book 3, Chapter 2, Section 34).
18. Edwin H. Palmer, *The Holy Spirit,* p. 59.
19. Kuyper, p. 76.
20. Geoffrey W. Bromiley, "The Bible Doctrine of Inspiration," *Christianity Today,* 4:139, November 23, 1959.
21. John F. Walvoord, "How Can Man Know God?" *Bibliotheca Sacra,* 116:105, April-June, 1959.
22. Daniel F. Fuller, "'Do We Need the Holy Spirit to Understand the Bible?" *Eternity,* 10:22, January, 1959.
23. Charles Hodge, *Systematic Theology,* 3:403.
24. J. Theodore Mueller, "The Holy Spirit and the Scriptures," *Revelation and the Bible,* p. 280.

25. Randolph Crump Miller, "The Holy Spirit and Christian Education," *Religious Education,* 57:178, May-June, 1962. Miller's italics.

PART 2

Chapter 4

1. Geoffrey F. Nuttall, *The Holy Spirit in Puritan Faith and Experience,* pp. 83-85.
2. Findley B. Edge, *Teaching for Results,* p. 19.
3. Clarence H. Benson, *The Christian Teacher,* p. 13.
4. Ibid., p. 63.
5. Ibid., p. 64.
6. Edge, p. 20.
7. Lois E. LeBar, *Education That Is Christian,* p. 230.

Chapter 5

1. John F. Walvoord, *The Holy Spirit,* p. 168.
2. Charles Caldwell Ryrie, *Biblical Theology of the New Testament,* p. 178.
3. Walvoord, pp. 165-66.
4. Ibid., pp. 173-88.
5. George Barker Stevens, *The Theology of the New Testament,* p. 434.
6. Walvoord, p. 176.
7. R. C. H. Lenski, *The Interpretation of St. Paul's First and Second Epistles to the Corinthians,* p. 490.
8. Lindsay Dewar, *The Holy Spirit and Modern Thought,* p. 67.
9. Walvoord, p. 75.
10. Ibid., p. 167.
11. Frank E. Gaebelein, *The Pattern of God's Truth,* p. 20.
12. Ibid., p. 23.
13. Albert Barnes, *Notes on the New Testament Explanatory and Practical, Thessalonians, Timothy, Titus, and Philemon,* p. 213.
14. Charles Caldwell Ryrie, "The Pauline Doctrine of the Church," *Bibliotheca Sacra,* 115:64, January-March, 1958.

Chapter 6

1. Harold C. Mason, *The Teaching Task of the Local Church,* p. 22.
2. Lois E. LeBar, *Education That Is Christian,* p. 236.
3. Augustus Hopkins Strong, *Systematic Theology,* p. 27.
4. LeBar, pp. 240-41.
5. Frank E. Gaebelein, *Christian Education in a Democracy,* p. 279.

Chapter 7

1. Clarence H. Benson, *The Christian Teacher,* p. 50.
2. Earle E. Cairns, "The Essence of Christian Higher Education," *Bibliotheca Sacra,* 111:344-45, October-December, 1954.

PART 3

Chapter 8

1. J. I. Packer, *"Fundamentalism" and the Word of God,* p. 42.
2. Joseph Foa Di Bruno, *Catholic Belief,* p. 24.

3. Bernard Ramm, *The Witness of the Spirit,* pp. 11, 12.
4. John Calvin, *The Deity of Christ and Other Sermons,* p. 243.
5. John Calvin, *Institutes of the Christian Religion,* I, 86 (Book 1, Chapter 7, Section 1).
6. Packer, p. 113.
7. John Dewey, *Experience and Education,* p. 4.
8. Ibid., pp. 4-5.
9. Lois E. LeBar, *Education That Is Christian,* p. 171.
10. Dewey, p. 17.
11. Charles E. S. Kraemer, "Relating Revelation to Education," *Presbyterian Action,* 8:6, April, 1958.
12. Harrison S. Elliott, *Can Religious Education Be Christian?,* p. 320.
13. Bernard Ramm, *The Pattern of Authority,* p. 76.
14. Auguste Sabatier, *Religions of Authority and the Religion of the Spirit,* p. 264.
15. Millar Burrows, *An Outline of Biblical Theology,* p. 50.
16. Balmer H. Kelly, "The Bible Is Witness and Instrument," *Presbyterian Action,* 8:10, 11, April, 1958.
17. Karl Barth, *The Holy Ghost and the Christian Life,* p. 39.
18. R. A. Finlayson, "Contemporary Views of Inspiration," *Revelation and the Bible,* p. 230.
19. William Temple, *Nature, Man and God,* p. 353.
20. James I. Packer, "Contemporary Views of Revelation," *Revelation and the Bible,* p. 95.
21. Herbert H. Framer, "The Bible: Its Significance and Authority," *The Interpreter's Bible,* 1:24.
22. Lewis Howard Grimes, "Christianity Is Learned through Living Encounter with the Bible," *The Minister and Christian Nurture,* p. 152.
23. George Park Fisher, *History of Christian Doctrine,* p. 11.
24. Packer, *"Fundamentalism" and the Word of God,* pp. 61-62.
25. Ramm, p. 36.
26. Ibid., p. 28.
27. J. N. Thomas, "The Authority of the Bible," *Theology Today,* 3:166, July, 1946.
28. Finlayson, p. 233.
29. Grimes, p. 144.
30. LeBar, p. 19.

Chapter 9

1. William Clayton Bower, "Religious Education Faces the Future," *The Journal of Religion,* 21:389, October, 1941.
2. George Albert Coe, *What Is Christian Education?,* chapter 3.
3. D. Campbell Wyckoff, *The Gospel and Christian Education,* p. 92.
4. Sara Little, *The Role of the Bible in Contemporary Christian Education,* p. 156.
5. Manuel Flores, "Biblical Theology in Christian Education," *World Christian Education,* 16:76, third quarter, 1961.
6. For more detail on the neoorthodox view of Christian education, see these articles by the author: "The Theological Bases of Neo-orthodox Christian Education," *Bibliotheca Sacra,* 119:161-69, April-June, 1962; and "The Educational Pattern of Neo-orthodox Christian Education," *Bibliotheca Sacra,* 119:342-51, October-December, 1962.

Chapter 10

1. H. C. G. Moule, *Veni Creator: Thoughts on the Person and Work of the Holy Spirit of Promise*, p. 63.
2. Joseph Parker, *The Paraclete*, p. 78.
3. Ibid., p. 83.
4. Lewis Sperry Chafer, *He That Is Spiritual*, p. 62.
5. Bernard Ramm, *The Pattern of Authority*, p. 37.
6. Bernard Ramm, *Protestant Biblical Interpretation*, p. 90.
7. J. I. Packer, *"Fundamentalism" and the Word of God*, p. 48.
8. Ramm, *Pattern of Authority*, p. 57. Ramm's italics.

PART 4

1. Clarence H. Benson, *The Christian Teacher*, p. 209.

Chapter 11

1. C. B. Eavey, *Principles of Teaching for Christian Teachers*, p. 46.
2. James DeForest Murch, *Christian Education and the Local Church*, p. 100.
3. Lois E. LeBar, *Education That Is Christian*, p. 220.
4. Ibid., p. 135.
5. Paul H. Vieth, *Teaching for Christian Living*, pp. 97, 98.
6. Paul H. Vieth, ed., *The Church and Christian Education*, pp. 74-75.
7. LeBar, p. 167.

Chapter 12

1. J. L. Corzine, *Looking at Learning*, p. 81.
2. Ibid., p. 80.
3. Findley B. Edge, *Teaching for Results*, p. 25.
4. G. Lester Anderson, "Basic Learning Theory for Teachers," *Educational Psychology*, p. 406.
5. Lois E. LeBar, *Education That Is Christian*, p. 147.
6. William F. Arndt and F. Wilbur Gingrich, *A Greek-English Lexicon of the New Testament and Other Early Christian Literature*, p. 491.
7. Charles A. Trentham, "Knowledge and the Holy Spirit," *The Baptist Student*, 7:31, April, 1957.
8. Lewis Sperry Chafer, *Systematic Theology*, 1:113.
9. S. A. Witmer, "Enduring Foundations in Education: The Other John," *United Evangelical Action*, 14:224, June 15, 1955.

Chapter 13

1. John Milton Gregory, *The Seven Laws of Teaching*, p. 2.
2. Findley B. Edge, *Teaching for Results*, p. 223. Edge's italics.
3. Ibid., p. 21.
4. Ronald C. Doll, "Shall We Close the Sunday Schools?" *Christianity Today*, 3:4, August 31, 1959.
5. Lewis Sperry Chafer, *He That Is Spiritual*, p. 63.

Chapter 14

1. Clarice M. Bowman, *Ways Youth Learn*, p. 8.
2. Robert A. Traina, *Methodical Bible Study*, p. 19.

3. L. Nelson Bell, "Teaching — Methods and Message," *Christianity Today,* 4:25, August 29, 1960.
4. Lois E. LeBar, *Education That Is Christian,* p. 219.
5. Carl F. H. Henry, "Pastors and Christian Education," *Christianity Today,* 3:29, August 31, 1959.
6. LeBar, pp. 222-23.
7. Ibid., p. 244.

PART 5

Chapter 15

1. Henry Barclay Swete, *The Holy Spirit in the Ancient Church,* p. 31.
2. Francis B. Denio, *The Supreme Leader,* p. 59.
3. Swete, p. 25.
4. Ibid., p. 34, *Tryph.* 4.
5. Ibid., p. 35, *Tryph.* 39.
6. Ibid, pp. 79, 80, *De monog.* 2.
7. Ibid., p. 87.
8. Ibid., p. 108.
9. R. Birch Hoyle, "Spirit (Holy), Spirit of God." *Encyclopedia of Religion and Ethics,* 11:802.
10. Swete, p. 168.
11. Augustus Neander, *Lectures on the History of Christian Dogmas,* 1:304.
12. C. R. B. Shapland, *The Letters of St. Athanasius Concerning the Holy Spirit,* p. 38.
13. Swete, p. 204.
14. Ibid., p. 334.
15. Ibid., p. 350.
16. John F. Walvoord, *The Holy Spirit,* p. 244.
17. John H. S. Burleigh, *Augustine: Earlier Writings,* xi, 38, p. 95.
18. Howard Grimes, "St. Augustine on Teaching," *Religious Education,* 54:173, March-April, 1959.
19. Walvoord, p. 246.
20. T. Rees, *The Holy Spirit in Thought and Experience,* p. 176.
21. Thomas Aquinas, "Reply to Objection 7," *De Magistro,* quoted in Kendig Brubaker Cully, ed., *Basic Writings in Christian Education,* p. 112.

Chapter 16

1. George Smeaton, *The Doctrine of the Holy Spirit,* p. 307.
2. John Calvin, *Institutes of the Christian Religion,* 1:348 (Book 2, Chapter 5, Section 5).
3. Smeaton, p. 313.
4. Regin Prenter, *Spiritus Creator,* trans. John M. Jensen (Philadelphia: Muhlenberg Press, 1953).
5. Ronald S. Wallace, *Calvin's Doctrine of the Word and Sacrament,* pp. 128-29.
6. Wilhelm Niesel, *The Theology of Calvin,* pp. 38-39.
7. Wallace, pp. 129-30.
8. Calvin, 2:622 (Book 4, Chapter 16, Section 19).
9. Benjamin B. Warfield, "Introductory Note" in *The Work of the Holy Spirit* by Abraham Kuyper, p. xxxiii.

10. Geoffrey F. Nuttall, *The Holy Spirit in Puritan Faith and Experience,* pp. 83-85.
11. Henry Bettenson ed., *Documents of the Christian Church,* p. 355.
12. Howard Watkin-Jones, *The Holy Spirit from Arminius to Wesley,* p. 186.
13. George Albert Coe, *What Is Christian Education?,* p. 33.
14. Frank E. Gaebelein, *Christian Education in a Democracy,* p. 219.
15. James D. Smart, *The Teaching Ministry of the Church,* p. 63.
16. Karl Barth, *The Holy Ghost and the Christian Life,* p. 45.
17. Harrison S. Elliott, *Can Religious Education Be Christian?,* p. 72.
18. Ibid., p. 73.
19. Ibid.
20. George A. Coe, "Religious Education Is in Peril," *International Journal of Religious Education,* 15:9, 10, January, 1939.
21. Sara Little, *The Role of the Bible in Contemporary Christian Education,* pp. 5, 165.
22. H. Shelton Smith, *Faith and Nurture,* p. 244.
23. For a critique of neoliberalism, see *Neo-liberalism,* by Robert Paul Lightner.

Summary

1. Lois E. LeBar, *Education That Is Christian,* p. 244.
2. Lewis Sperry Chafer, *Systematic Theology,* 1:113.
3. LeBar, p. 238.
4. L. Nelson Bell, "Teaching — Methods and Message," *Christianity Today,* 4:25, August 29, 1960.
5. Kenneth S. Kantzer, "Calvin and the Holy Scriptures," *Inspiration and Interpretation,* pp. 130-37.

Bibliography

COMMENTARIES AND LEXICONS

Alford, Henry. *The Greek Testament.* 4 vols. London: Rivingtons, 1859.

Arndt, William F., and F. Wilbur Gingrich. *A Greek-English Lexicon of the New Testament and Other Early Christian Literature.* Chicago: U. of Chicago, 1957.

Barnes, Albert. *Notes on the New Testament Explanatory and Practical, Luke and John.* Ed. Robert Frew. Grand Rapids: Baker, 1949.

———. *Notes on the New Testament Explanatory and Practical, Thessalonians, Timothy, Titus, and Philemon.* Ed. Robert Frew. Grand Rapids: Baker, 1949.

Cremer, Hermann. *Biblico-Theological Lexicon of New Testament Greek.* Trans. William Urwick. 4th Eng. ed. Edinburgh: T. & T. Clark, 1895.

Delitzsch, Franz. *Biblical Commentary on the Prophecies of Isaiah.* Trans. James Martin. 2 vols. Grand Rapids: Eerdmans, 1950.

Dods, Marcus. "The Gospel of St. John." In *The Expositor's Greek Testament,* ed. W. Robertson Nicoll, vol. 1. Grand Rapids: Eerdmans, 1951.

Findlay, G. G. "St. Paul's First Epistle to the Corinthians." In *The Expositor's Greek Testament,* ed. W. Robertson Nicoll, vol. 2 Grand Rapids: Eerdmans, 1951.

Lange, John Peter. "John." In *Lange's Commentary on the Holy Scriptures,* trans. and ed. Philip Schaff. Reprint. Grand Rapids: Zondervan, n.d.

175

Lenski, R. C. H. *The Interpretation of St. John's Gospel.* Columbus, O.: Lutheran Book Concern, 1942.

———. *The Interpretation of St. Paul's First and Second Epistles to the Corinthians.* Columbus, O.: Wartburg, 1946.

———. *The Interpretation of the Epistles of St. Peter, St. John and St. Jude.* Columbus, O.: Wartburg, 1945.

Plummer, A. "The Epistles of St. John, with Notes, Introduction and Appendices." In *Cambridge Greek Testament for Schools and Colleges,* ed. J. J. S. Perowne. Cambridge: U. Press, 1886.

Robertson, Archibald Thomas. *Word Pictures in the New Testament.* 6 vols. Nashville: Broadman, 1930.

Ryle, John Charles. *Expository Thoughts on John.* 3 vols. London: William Hunt, 1883.

Salmond, S. D. F. "The Epistle to the Ephesians." In *The Expositor's Greek Testament,* ed. W. Robertson Nicoll, vol. 3. Grand Rapids: Eerdmans, 1951.

Thayer, Joseph Henry. *A Greek-English Lexicon of the New Testament.* 4th ed. Edinburgh, T. & T. Clark, 1901.

Westcott, Brooke Foss. *The Gospel According to St. John: The Authorised Version with Introduction and Notes.* London: John Murray, 1890.

Wuest, Kenneth S. *In These Last Days.* Grand Rapids: Eerdmans, 1957.

THEOLOGICAL WORKS

Bettenson, Henry., ed. *Documents of the Christian Church.* New York: Oxford U. Press, 1954.

Burleigh, John H. S. *Augustine: Earlier Writings.* Sel. and trans. John H. S. Burleigh. Philadelphia: Westminster, 1953.

Burrows, Millar. *An Outline of Biblical Theology.* Philadelphia: Westminster, 1945.

Calvin, John. *Institutes of the Christian Religion.* Trans. John Allen. 2 vols. Philadelphia: Presbyterian Bd. of Christian Ed. 1936.

———. *The Deity of Christ and Other Sermons.* Trans. LeRoy Nixon. Grand Rapids: Eerdmans, 1950.

Chafer, Lewis Sperry. *He That Is Spiritual.* Wheaton: Van Kampen, 1918.

——————. *Systematic Theology.* 8 vols. Dallas: Dallas Seminary, 1947.

Di Bruno, Joseph Foa. *Catholic Belief.* 2d. rev. ed. London: Burns & Oates, 1878.

Fisher, George Park. *History of Christian Doctrine.* 7th impression. Edinburgh: T. & T. Clark, 1949.

Gaussen, L. *The Inspiration of the Holy Scriptures.* Chicago: Moody, 1949.

Hodge, Charles. *Systematic Theology.* 3 vols. New York: Scribner, 1883.

Lightner, Robert Paul. *Neo-liberalism.* Chicago: Regular Bapt., 1959.

Neander, Augustus. *Lectures on the History of Christian Dogmas.* Trans. J. E. Ryland. 2 vols. London: Bell & Daldy, 1866.

Niesel, Wilhelm. *The Theology of Calvin.* Trans. Harold Knight. Philadelphia: Westminster, 1956.

Packer, J. I. *"Fundamentalism" and the Word of God.* Grand Rapids: Eerdmans, 1958.

Ramm, Bernard. *Protestant Biblical Interpretation.* Boston: W. A. Wilde, 1950.

——————. *The Pattern of Authority.* Grand Rapids: Eerdmans, 1957.

Ryrie, Charles Caldwell. *Biblical Theology of the New Testament.* Chicago: Moody, 1959.

Sabatier, Auguste. *Religions of Authority and the Religion of the Spirit.* Trans. L. S. Houghton. New York: McClure, 1904.

Stevens, George Barker. *The Theology of the New Testament.* 2d. rev. ed. Edinburgh: T. & T. Clark, 1918.

Strong, Augustus Hopkins. *Systematic Theology.* 12th ed. Philadelphia: Judson, 1907.

Temple, William. *Nature, Man and God.* New York: Macmillan, 1949.

Wallace, Ronald S. *Calvin's Doctrine of the Word and Sacrament.* Grand Rapids: Eerdmans, 1957.

Wuest, Kenneth S. *The Practical Use of the Greek New Testament.* Chicago: Moody, 1946.

BOOKS ON THE HOLY SPIRIT

Barth, Karl. *The Holy Ghost and the Christian Life.* Trans. R. Birch Hoyle. London: Frederick Muller, 1938.

Biederwolf, W. E. *Help to the Study of the Holy Spirit.* 4th ed. New York: Revell, 1903.

Clemance, Clement. *The Scripture Doctrine of the Holy Spirit.* London: John Snow, 1887.

Denio, Francis B. *The Supreme Leader.* Boston: Pilgrim, 1900.

Dewar, Lindsay. *The Holy Spirit and Modern Thought.* New York: Harper, 1959.

Hare, Julius Charles. *The Mission of the Comforter.* 2d. London ed. Boston: Gould & Lincoln, 1854.

Kuyper, Abraham. *The Work of the Holy Spirit.* Trans. Henri DeVries, Grand Rapids: Eerdmans, 1956.

Moule, H. C. G. *Veni Creator: Thoughts on the Person and Work of the Holy Spirit of Promise.* London: Hodder & Stoughton, 1890.

Murray, Andrew. *The Spirit of Christ: Thoughts on the Indwelling of the Holy Spirit in the Believer and the Church.* London: Nisbet, n.d.

Nuttall, Geoffrey F. *The Holy Spirit in Puritan Faith and Experience.* Oxford: Basil Blackwell, 1946.

Palmer, Edwin H. *The Holy Spirit.* Grand Rapids: Baker, 1958.

Parker, Joseph. *The Paraclete.* New York: Scribner, Armstrong & Co., 1875.

Prenter, Regin. *Spiritus Creator.* Trans. John M. Jensen. Philadelphia: Muhlenberg, 1953.

Ramm, Bernard. *The Witness of the Spirit.* Grand Rapids: Eerdmans, 1959.

Rees, T. *The Holy Spirit in Thought and Experience.* New York: Scribner, 1915.

Robinson, Henry Wheeler. *The Christian Experience of the Holy Spirit.* London: Nisbet, 1928.

Shapland, C. R. B. *The Letters of St. Athanasius Concerning the Holy Spirit.* London: Epworth, 1951.

Simpson, Albert Benjamin. *The Holy Spirit.* 2 vols. New York: Christian Alliance, 1895.

Smeaton, George. *The Doctrine of the Holy Spirit.* Edinburgh: T. & T. Clark, 1882.

Swete, Henry Barclay. *The Holy Spirit in the Ancient Church.* London: Macmillan, 1912.

———. *The Holy Spirit in the New Testament.* London: Macmillan, 1909.

Walvoord, John F. *The Holy Spirit.* Wheaton: Van Kampen, 1954.

Watkin-Jones, Howard. *The Holy Spirit from Arminius to Wesley.* London: Epworth, 1929.

BOOKS ON CHRISTIAN EDUCATION

Benson, Clarence H. *The Christian Teacher.* Chicago: Moody, 1950.

Bowman, Clarice M. *Ways Youth Learn.* New York: Harper, 1952.

Coe, George Albert. *What Is Christian Education?* New York: Scribner, 1929.

Corzine, J. L. *Looking at Learning.* Nashville: Sunday School Board of Southern Bapt. Convention, 1934.

Cully, Kendig Brubaker., ed. *Basic Writings in Christian Education.* Philadelphia: Westminster, 1960.

Dewey, John. *Experience and Education.* New York: Macmillan, 1938.

Eavey, C. B. *Principles of Teaching for Christian Teachers.* 4th ed. Grand Rapids: Zondervan, 1940.

Edge, Findley B. *Teaching for Results.* Nashville: Broadman, 1956.

Elliott, Harrison S. *Can Religious Education Be Christian?* New York: Macmillan, 1949.

Gaebelein, Frank E. *Christian Education in a Democracy.* New York: Oxford U. Press, 1951.

———. *The Pattern of God's Truth.* New York: Oxford U. Press, 1954.

Gregory, John Milton. *The Seven Laws of Teaching.* Grand Rapids: Baker, 1955.

LeBar, Lois E. *Education That Is Christian.* New York: Revell, 1958.

Little, Sara. *The Role of the Bible in Contemporary Christian Education.* Richmond, Va.: Knox, 1961.

Mason, Harold C. *The Teaching Task of the Local Church.* Winona Lake, Ind.: Light & Life, 1960.

Murch, James DeForest. *Christian Education and the Local Church.* Rev. ed. 1958. Cincinnati, O.: Standard, 1943.

Smart, James D. *The Teaching Ministry of the Church.* Philadelphia: Westminster, 1954.

Smith, H. Shelton. *Faith and Nurture.* New York: Scribner, 1941.

Traina, Robert A. *Methodical Bible Study.* New York: Ganis & Harris, 1952.

Vieth, Paul H. *Teaching for Christian Living.* 3d. ed. St. Louis: Bethany Press, 1929.

──────. *The Church and Christian Education.* St. Louis: Bethany Press, 1947.

Wyckoff, D. Campbell. *The Gospel and Christian Education.* Philadelphia: Westminster, 1959.

ENCYCLOPEDIA AND ESSAY ARTICLES

Anderson, G. Lester. "Basic Learning Theory for Teachers." In *Educational Psychology,* ed. Charles E. Skinner, 4th ed. Englewood Cliffs, N.J.: Prentice-Hall, 1959.

Finlayson, R. A. "Contemporary Views of Inspiration." In *Revelation and the Bible,* ed., Carl F. H. Henry. Grand Rapids: Baker, 1958.

Framer, Herbert H. "The Bible: Its Significance and Authority." In *The Interpreter's Bible,* vol. 1. New York: Abingdon-Cokesbury, 1952.

Grimes, Lewis Howard. "Christianity Is Learned through Living Encounter with the Bible." In *The Minister and Christian Nurture,* ed. Nathaniel Frederick Forsyth. New York: Abingdon, 1957.

Henry, Carl F. H. "Divine Revelation and the Bible." In *Inspiration and Interpretation,* ed. John F. Walvoord, Grand Rapids: Eerdmans, 1957.

Hoyle, R. Birch. "Spirit (Holy), Spirit of God." In *Encyclopedia of Religion and Ethics*, ed. James Hastings, vol. 11. New York: Scribner, 1951.

Kantzer, Kenneth S. "Calvin and the Holy Scriptures." In *Inspiration and Interpretation*, ed. John F. Walvoord. Grand Rapids: Eerdmans, 1957.

Mueller, J. Theodore. "The Holy Spirit and the Scriptures." In *Revelation and the Bible*, ed. Carl F. H. Henry. Grand Rapids: Baker, 1958.

Mullins, E. Y. "Paraclete." In *The International Standard Bible Encyclopedia*, ed. James Orr, vol. 4. Grand Rapids: Eerdmans, 1949.

Packer, James I. "Contemporary Views of Revelation." In *Revelation and the Bible*, ed. Carl F. H. Henry. Grand Rapids: Baker, 1958.

PERIODICALS

Bell, L. Nelson. "Teaching — Methods and Message." *Christianity Today* 4(Aug. 29, 1960):25.

Bower, William Clayton. "Religious Education Faces the Future." *The Journal of Religion* 21(1951):385-97.

Bromiley, Geoffrey W. "The Bible Doctrine of Inspiration." *Christianity Today* 4(Nov. 23, 1959):138-39.

Cairns, Earl C. "The Essence of Christian Higher Education." *Bibliotheca Sacra* 3(1954):338-45.

Coe, George A. "Religious Education Is in Peril." *International Journal of Religious Education* 15(1939):9.

Doll, Ronald C. "Shall We Close the Sunday Schools?" *Christianity Today* 3(Aug. 31, 1959):3-5.

Flores, Manuel. "Biblical Theology in Christian Education." *World Christian Education* 16(1961):76.

Fuller, Daniel F. "Do We need the Holy Spirit to Understand the Bible?" *Eternity* 10(Jan. 1959):22.

Grimes, Howard. "St. Augustine on Teaching." *Religious Education* 54(1959):171-76.

Henry, Carl F. H. "Pastors and Christian Education." *Christianity Today* 3(Aug. 31, 1959):29-30.

Kelly, Balmer, H. "The Bible Is Witness and Instrument." *Presbyterian Action* 8(Apr. 1958):10-11.

Kraemer, Charles E. S. "Relating Revelation to Education." *Presbyterian Action* 8(Apr. 1958):6-7.

Miller, Randolph Crump. "The Holy Spirit and Christian Education." *Religious Education* 57(1962):178-84, 237-38.

Ryrie, Charles Caldwell. "The Pauline Doctrine of the Church." *Bibliotheca Sacra* 115(1958):62-67.

Thomas, J. N. "The Authority of the Bible." *Theology Today,* 3(1946):166.

Trentham, Charles A. "Knowledge and the Holy Spirit." *The Baptist Student* 7(Apr. 1957):30-32.

Walvoord, John F. "How Can Man Know God?" *Bibliotheca Sacra* 116(1959):99-108.

Witmer, S. A. "Enduring Foundations in Education: The Other John." *United Evangelical Action* 14(1955):223-24, 231.

Zuck, Roy B. "Why Do Teens Quit Church?" *Link* 11(Jan. 1963):6.

————. "The Educational Pattern of Neo-orthodox Christian Education." *Bibliotheca Sacra* 119(1962):342-51.

————. "The Theological Bases of Neo-orthodox Christian Education." *Bibliotheca Sacra* 119(1962):161-69.

Subject Index

Albertus Magnus, 150
Albigenses, 150
Arius, 147
Athanasius, 147
Augustine, 148-50
Authority
  Bible as, 98-103, 139, 151
  Christ as, 101
  church as, 91-93
  educational experience as, 94-96
  existential encounter as, 97-98
  God as ultimate, 99
  pattern of, 102
  religious experience as, 93, 95-96, 97
  teachers as, 93-94
  in teaching, 90, 91-104

Barclay, Robert, 154
Barth, Karl, 55
Basil of Caesarea, 147
Bernard of Clairvaux, 150
Bible
  animation of, 20, 22
  appropriation of, 20, 22
  authority of, 15-16, 42, 98-103, 112, 152
  basic content in Christian education, 15-16, 17, 104-11, 159-60, 163
  canon of, 43
  divine origin of, 15-16, 152
  enlightens, 20
  finality of, 102 155, 157
  as foundation of curriculum, 14, 19, 90, 102, 103, 107
  generates faith, 20
  and Holy Spirit, 20-22, 42-45, 102, 112, 113, 152, 153, 159
  infallible, 42, 95, 100
  inspiration of, 20-21, 36, 42-44, 99
  interpretation of, 100, 112-115
  knowledge of, 119-20

  and neoorthodoxy, 97-98, 110, 111, 152, 157-58
  nurtures, 21
  as objective truth, 55, 152
  operative efficaciousness of, 22
  place of in Christian education, 90, 104
  and pupils' experiences, 16, 95-96, 163
  revelation of God, 43, 52, 95-96
  source of Christian education principles, 102-3
  and teachers, 83, 88
Blindness, spiritual, 21, 51, 131
Boehme, Jocob, 154
Brunner, Emil, 157-58

Calvin, John, 22, 151, 152
Carlstadt, 152
Carnality
  and Bible interpretation, 113
  hindrance to learning, 131-32
  of pupils, 22, 34, 55
  of teachers, 19
Cathari, 150
Christ
  as authority, 101
  center of curriculum, 107-8
  center of one's life, 120-21
  and Holy Spirit, 25-30
  as Intercessor, 29, 108
  liberals' concept of, 155
  master Teacher, 132
  source of teachers' strength, 108
  teaching His disciples, 36-37
Christian education
  aims of, 18, 64-65, 119-22, 163-64
  and Bible, 15-17, 90, 98-111
  curriculum, 90, 102, 107-11, 140-42
  distinctives of, 14-22, 163
  divine nature of, 18, 161-62

183

Scripture Index